Standard Basque and

The origins of Basque dialects, a highly disputed area of research in Basque studies, are examined.

The author, the foremost expert on Basque dialects, traces their emergence to medieval times, using: a) the profusion of features common to all dialects: b) the large number of innovations common to all dialects; and c) the fact that the only truly divergent dialects are the western and Souletin ones. In contrast, the three central dialects differ in far fewer and less important respects.

The main contribution of *Standard Basque and Its Dialects* to the scholarly debate about the formation of Basque is that it identifies the nuclei from which the current dialects almost certainly emerged. The book explains the points of view that Basque speakers have upheld concerning their dialects, the formation of provincial standards starting in the eighteenth century, and the launch of Standard Basque in the second half of the twentieth century.

Koldo Zuazo is a Basque linguist, professor at the University of the Basque Country and specialist in Basque language dialectology and sociolinguistics. His main contribution has been the study and classification of Basque dialects and the indication of their possible places of origin. He has worked on the formation of Standard Basque.

Gregor Benton is a student of Basque and Emeritus Professor of Chinese history at Cardiff University. He has translated books from many languages.

Standard Basque and Its Dialects

Koldo Zuazo

**Translated by
Gregor Benton**

Routledge
Taylor & Francis Group

LONDON AND NEW YORK

First published 2019
by Routledge
2 Park Square, Milton Park, Abingdon, Oxon OX14 4RN

and by Routledge
605 Third Avenue, New York, NY 10017

First issued in paperback 2022

Routledge is an imprint of the Taylor & Francis Group, an informa business

Publisher's Note
The publisher has gone to great lengths to ensure the quality of this reprint but points out that some imperfections in the original copies may be apparent.

Translation © 2019 Gregor Benton

British Library Cataloguing in Publication Data
A catalogue record for this book is available from the British Library

Library of Congress Cataloging-in-Publication Data
Names: Zuazo, Koldo, author. | Benton, Gregor, translator.
Title: Standard Basque and its dialects / Koldo Zuazo ; translated by Gregor Benton.
Other titles: Euskera y sus dialectos. English
Description: Milton Park, Abingdon, Oxon ; New York, NY : Routledge, 2019. | Includes bibliographical references and index.
Identifiers: LCCN 2018036846 | ISBN 9781138367548 (hardback) | ISBN 9780429429729 (ebook)
Subjects: LCSH: Basque language--Dialects.
Classification: LCC PH5187 .Z8313 2019 | DDC 499/.927--dc23
LC record available at https://lccn.loc.gov/2018036846

ISBN: 978-1-03-240171-3 (pbk)
ISBN: 978-1-138-36754-8 (hbk)
ISBN: 978-0-429-42972-9 (ebk)

DOI: 10.4324/9780429429729

Typeset in Times New Roman
by Taylor & Francis Books

To the sculptor and creator Jorge Oteiza (1908–2003), for his contribution to rescuing Basque culture from the "void" and presenting it to the world

Contents

Illustrations

Figures

Table

Introduction

The University of the Basque Country is a relatively young institution, born in 1980. This late date might surprise some, given the dense population of the Basque Country and its high level of economic development. The reason lies in large part in the Spanish Civil War, after which the victors imposed a long and severe punishment on the vanquished. As a result, hundreds of young Basques had to move every year to Valladolid, Salamanca, or Zaragoza to pursue their university degrees. As for the youth of the Basque provinces in the French state, they attended – and continue to attend – universities in Pau, Toulouse, or Bordeaux.

True, there were two private universities, one run by the Jesuits of Deusto, in Bilbao, and the other by Opus Dei in Iruña (Pamplona), but neither offered courses relevant to the Basque Country – including its language, a field in which the lack of university research that might develop and invigorate its study and train specialists in it was sorely missed.

It is also true that the creation, in 1948, of a chair in the Basque language at the University of Bordeaux and of a second chair, in 1952, at the University of Salamanca had positive consequences. However, this was not enough to promote research and channel it in the necessary direction.

The intervention of some well-known international linguists also helped establish Basque studies. International scholarly attention started early, in the sixteenth century, and has continued until this day. In the second half of the twentieth century, for example, René Lafon, Antonio Tovar, Rudolf de Rijk, and Larry Trask were among those who contributed most to the study of Basque and to its spread across the world. Even so, their contribution was insufficient.

Within the Basque Country, linguistic studies have tended to be a church concern. One cannot but acknowledge the good will and high seriousness that many ecclesiastical scholars have devoted to this endeavour. Nevertheless, given the minimal linguistic expertise acquired in the seminaries and convents, their work too has failed to raise Basque studies to the same level as those of other languages.

It is a fact that, for all these and other reasons, Basque has become the object of a host of myths and legends that result in its portrayal as an enigmatic and mysterious language.

In this book, I set out to bring to public attention some of the results achieved over the last few years in linguistic research, starting with the birth of the Departments of Basque Philology after the death of the dictator Francisco Franco. My specific aim is to tackle various themes related to the study of standardisation and the Basque dialects.

The book comprises six chapters. Chapter 1 sketches the history of Basque, in order to provide the necessary context for a proper understanding of the issues under discussion. One of the consequences that can be drawn from this brief sketch is that the current weakness of the language, and the shrinking of its domain across the centuries, has not been due to a lack of interest or to neglect on the part of the Basques themselves, as many have claimed. On the contrary, as with most of the world's endangered languages, Basque's debilitation and decline are due to the language policies adopted by governments. We know that as early as the sixteenth century, governments were already taking measures to restrict Basque. The Nueva Planta decree of 1716, in Spain, and the reforms carried out after the Revolution of 1789 in France were decisive in promoting the ascendancy of Castilian and French, to the extent that they marginalised other languages, including Basque. The diversification of Basque into dialects is also, in large measure, a consequence of policies of linguistic marginalisation.

Chapter 2 considers the origins of the dialects. This subject is dominated by a deeply rooted misconception. Up until recently, the general view was that the present-day dialects reflect tribal divisions from the pre-Roman period. Here, in contrast, I defend a very different thesis, first propounded by the linguist Koldo Mitxelena. Like him, I believe that today's dialects almost certainly originated in the Middle Ages.

Chapter 3 seeks to identify the precise foci around which the dialects arose. I argue that Iruña (Pamplona in Spanish), the most important Basque city in ancient times, was probably the initial focus. Later, Gasteiz (Vitoria in Spanish) probably played a major role in the West, a role never previously acknowledged. The central zone of Bizkaia (Biscay), also in the West, the provinces of Zuberoa (Soule in French) and Lower Navarre, in the East, and the Gipuzkoan region of Beterri, which lies between Tolosa and Donostia (San Sebastián in Spanish), have also served as innovatory centres.

Chapter 4 examines how Basques have viewed their dialects. In the eighteenth century, Manuel Larramendi declared that the Basque dialects, divine in nature, were an authentic fount of riches that must be cultivated and protected – thus propagating what became an abiding myth about the language. There was also a contrary thesis – that the dialects were vulgar and degenerate forms of speech that made communication between speakers of Basque difficult or impossible and could therefore play no role in the adaptation of Basque to the necessities of modern life.

Chapter 5 describes the five literary dialects of the Basque Country. It will be seen that their constitution and development are closely related to the myth invented by Larramendi and the defence of the dialects. At the same time, I will describe two linguistic experiments devised in the late nineteenth century in Bizkaia which, in my opinion, have had truly lamentable consequences for the language: purism, and what I call "the reconstruction of original Basque."

Finally, Chapter 6 starts with a brief description of the history of the standardisation of Basque. I explain why this did not happen until late, starting in 1964, and demonstrate the bases upon which the present model of a standard language was erected.

This book is meant not just for linguists but for everyone interested in language and particularly in Basque. I have therefore tried to keep technical terms to a minimum. However, Chapters 2 and 3 require some knowledge of linguistic terms and concepts, so I have added a glossary and indicated relevant terms in the text by adding an asterisk to the right of them. These two chapters differ from the rest, but the materials they present are more novel in character.

This book is a synthesis and at the same time a further elaboration of existing studies, published in Basque and developed with the help of José Ignacio Hualde, of the University of Illinois, and my friends and colleagues Xabier Artiagoitia and Ernesto Pastor Díaz de Garayo at the University of the Basque Country. Nahia Grande helped me with the maps. I would like to express my sincere thanks to all these people.

1 Basque's survival

The origin of Basque is a principal issue in Basque studies. Another, no less important issue, is why Basque has survived. Basque and its precursors managed to stay alive despite pressure from Indo-European languages, Latin, and the dialects that emerged from Latin, including Occitan, Navarrese Romance (a variety of Navarro-Aragonese, now extinct), French, and Castilian.

That Basque survived these assaults is a cause for rejoicing – on the part of its speakers, who have defended it so tenaciously, and of all humanity, for whom Basque is part of a universal linguistic heritage and provides unique evidence of the nature and structure of language.

Basque has persisted despite geographic shrinkage, social marginalisation (both now and in the past), profound changes in its internal structure, and extreme dialectal fragmentation, as I go on to show.

Geographic shrinkage

We know little or nothing about the geographic extent of Basque in antiquity. We can only hazard some guesses about the situation at the time when the Roman Empire established a hold on the region, 200 years before the beginning of the common era. In those days, Basque seems to have occupied a broad stretch of territory in the southwest of what is now France. It coincided, more or less, with the course of the Garonne river, which originates in the Aran Valley (Val d'Aran), in the Catalan province of Lleida, and meets the sea north of Bordeaux. This Basque-speaking territory therefore corresponded to what until 2016 was the French administrative region of Aquitaine. Epigraphs found in the region, written in Latin in the first to third centuries, contain the names of people and divinities that are in many cases structurally similar or identical to present-day Basque (see Gorrochategui 1984, 1995).

To the south, the territory where Basque was spoken probably extended to regions that are today part of the provinces of Burgos, La Rioja, Soria, Zaragoza, and Huesca in the Spanish state. Toponymic evidence suggests that Basque was almost certainly spoken in places close to the Pyrenees, on both the French and the Spanish side, at least as far south as the Aran Valley.

We do not know when Basque was finally lost to these areas. In some places the loss must have happened during the period of Roman rule, but in others Basque survived much longer. We have only two pieces of evidence regarding areas in which Basque was spoken in the remote past. We know that in the first half of the thirteenth century, between 1234 and 1239, King Fernando III of Castile conceded a *fuero* (a charter or code of laws) to the inhabitants of the Ojacastro Valley in La Rioja, allowing the use of Basque in courts. Here is a text regarding the event, in which Don Moriel, the Merino Mayor of Castile, and the Mayor of Ojacastro played leading roles (Merino Urrutia 1978: 18):

> The mayor of Ojacastro, asked to bring in Don Morial who was Merino (Chief Law-Enforcement Officer) of Castile, so he would know that a man from Ojacastro had the right to reply in Basque if he was sued by another man from the town or from outside of the town. Thus Don Morial came to know that the inhabitants of Ojacastro had this *fuero*.[1]

On the other hand, as José María Lacarra has shown (Irigarai 1974: 115), the municipal ordinances of Huesca in 1349 prohibited the use of Arabic, Hebrew, and Basque in the local market, suggesting that Basque was in fact used by traders in that northern Aragonese city:

> Let no merchant be employed who does any trading, who buys or sells with anyone speaking in Arabic, or in Hebrew, or in Basque; and whoever does it, should pay 30 *solidi* as a fine.[2]

However, none of this evidence is definitive. In some cases, the Basque population might have expanded beyond its original territory in more recent times, by populating new areas or repopulating old ones, perhaps as a consequence of the expulsion of the Arabs.

Starting in the sixteenth century, more copious and reliable evidence is available, as I now go on to show.

Basque in the sixteenth century

It seems that by the sixteenth century the area in which Basque was spoken had shrunk into the seven Basque provinces of the present day: Lapurdi (Labourd in French), Lower Navarre, and Zuberoa (Soule in French) on French territory, and Araba (Álava in Spanish), Bizkaia (Biscay), Gipuzkoa, and Navarre on Spanish territory. These provinces were not entirely Basque-speaking. The western part of Bizkaia, to the west of Bilbao, and the southern territories of Araba and Navarre, used Romance (a generic name for languages derived from Latin), as did Baiona (Bayonne in French) and the surrounding area in Lapurdi. On the other hand, people in some border regions that were not administratively part of the Basque Country spoke Basque. Today, one example is Eskiula (Esquiule) in the former French province of Béarn.

There were also hybrid languages, or pidgins, based in part on Basque. One pidgin was a mixture of Icelandic and Basque, another of Basque and various aboriginal Canadian languages. The Basque coast was a veritable fishing and whaling power in earlier times, and Basque traders and seafarers were active far and wide.

In 1937, the Dutchman Nicolaas Deen published an extensive vocabulary of Basque-Icelandic Pidgin, including entire sentences in the language (Deen 1937). We know next to nothing about the Basque-Canadian pidgins, whose scant remnants have been recovered and researched by another Dutchman, Peter Bakker (1991). However, the existence of this pidgin is attested in various primary sources. For example, the Gipuzkoan chronicler and historian Esteban Garibai, in his *Compendio historial*, published in 1571 (Zubiaur 1990: 135–6), wrote:

> Navigators of the province of Gipuzkoa, the dominion of Bizkaia, and the Basque lands [Lapurdi] went once a year to Newfoundland to fish for cod and hunt whales, and the savages of that region got to know their language, despite the brevity of their annual communication, which lasted less than two months.[3]

The French inquisitor Pierre Lancre (1553–1631), who ordered so many Basques to be burned at the stake, also collected testimony regarding the relations between fishers and traders from the Lapurdian coast with inhabitants of Canada (Lancre 1613 [2004]: 32–3):

> They were delighted to find, even before they became familiar with those places, that the Basques were already trafficking there, even to the point that the Canadians negotiated with the French in no other language than that of the Basques.[4]

The Basque-speaking region starting in the sixteenth century

Starting in the sixteenth century, the Basque language suffered a never-ending series of setbacks, especially in Araba and Navarre. In the course of the eighteenth century, the Spanish Crown took measures against all languages other than Castilian. An example is the Nueva Planta decree of 1716, promulgated by Felipe V of Bourbon, which established Spanish as the only language of the courts of law and government, mostly at the expense of Catalan. In the nineteenth century, the Basque Country was ravaged by the Carlist wars of 1833–39 and 1872–76. The long years of military dictatorship following the Civil War of 1936–39, until the death of Franco in 1975, were similarly devastating, and brought Basque to the brink of extinction.

In 1973, a study appeared that quantified the total number of Basque speakers (Irizar 1973). Its author, Pedro Irizar, counted around 610,000 Basque speakers, of whom only 532000 lived in Basque-speaking areas. The rest were emigrants who had settled in Madrid, Barcelona, Paris, Pau, Bordeaux, various parts of the Americas, and other places. The number of speakers was shown to have fallen greatly, calling into question the language's very continuity under the social conditions of the late twentieth century.

A closer look at the figures suggests that the situation was even worse than it appeared at first sight. For example, in Eibar, my place of birth, the number of Basque speakers was around 11,000, out of a total population of 37,073. One third of the population knew Basque, but only the older ones, above the age of 40–45, especially men, used it as a matter of routine in their daily lives. Younger people spoke above all in Castilian and used Basque only at home and when speaking to older people. In many families, the parents found it hard to speak Castilian, whereas the children were unable to construct a full sentence in Basque. Basque had attracted the stigma of a "rural language," which did not help at a time when much of the Basque Country was beginning to industrialise. What was true of Eibar was also true of other urban nuclei in Gipuzkoa and Bizkaia, such as Tolosa, Beasain, Ordizia, Urretxu, Zumarraga, Legazpi, Oñati, Arrasate, Elgoibar, Durango, and Amorebieta.

Table 1.1 shows the distribution of Basque speakers by province in the early 1970s:

Table 1.1 Basque speakers by province

Province	Basque speakers
Gipuzkoa	276,843
Bizkaia	140,229
Lapurdi	39,530
Navarre	35,228
Lower Navarre	27,016
Zuberoa and Béarn	11,907
Araba	1,863
Total	532,616

The situation in Araba was particularly critical. Only 1,863 of its inhabitants were thought to know Basque, including residents in industrial centres such as Agurain (Salvatierra in Spanish), Araia, and the capital Vitoria-Gasteiz, who had moved there from neighbouring Basque provinces. Of the 1,863 Basque speakers in Araba, 1,432 lived in Aramaio, at the intersection of Gipuzkoa and Bizkaia, while the remaining 431 were scattered across Zigoitia, Legutio, Baranbio, and Laudio, at the same intersection. In Araba as in the whole of the Basque Country, the disappearance of Basque seemed to be an imminent and irreversible fact of the post-war period.

Basque's recovery

A few years before Pedro Irizar published his survey, in around 1960, the first symptoms became apparent of a change that, in the course of just a few years, produced surprising results. On the one hand, schools arose, the *ikastolak*, which functioned exclusively in Basque. At first, the classes were given in private houses, semi-clandestinely, but later they were able to use premises made available by the Church or other entities, and in time they were in a position to build or equip real schools.

The advent of these new centres of learning meant that the creation of a standard language could no longer be delayed, so that textbooks and other necessary materials could be prepared and distributed. The first sketch of the new norm was published in 1964, and, starting in 1968, the Academy of the Basque Language decided to intervene, against the opposition of many of its members.

In around 1965, the first centres for Basque adult education were set up: *gau eskolak* or night schools, which later acquired the name *euskaltegi* or centres of Basque schooling. Thanks to these centres, people from outside the Basque Country or Basques whose parents had not transmitted the language to them could learn it, or at least acquire a certain level of linguistic competence.

Apart from these three important achievements, the creation of schools for children and adults and the elaboration of standard Basque, the language made a few small breakthroughs in communications media (radio and magazines), under the tutelage and control of the Church. In the literary field, another important change was brought about: Basque made the transition from a predominantly rural literature depicting or interpreting local everyday life, mannerisms, and customs (*literatura costumbrista*) to a literature more in accord with the new reality of the Basque Country, predominantly urban and industrial. Popular music also underwent a marked change, in both its lyrics and its tunes, and became better connected to the feelings of young Basques. The group Ez Dok Amairu (1965–1972), in which singers and other artists worked together, had a big impact in those years on Basque society.

As a result of all these changes, starting in 1970 the language began to manifest symptoms of recovery. This happened, to a greater or a lesser extent, across the whole Basque Country, including in places from which Basque had long disappeared. In time, the experience was translated across the frontiers of the Basque Country, and Basque classes started up in Basque centres throughout the world: Madrid, Barcelona, Valladolid, Paris, Pau, Bordeaux, London, Uruguay, Argentina, Chile, Mexico, and various places in the United States.

The social marginalisation of Basque

Basque in the south of the Basque Country

It seems clear that, in the life of a language, the decline in the domains in which it is used does even greater harm than its loss of geographic space. This is certainly true of Basque. For example, Basque never featured in documents of the Kingdom of Navarre, which were written at first in Latin and later in Navarrese Romance and Castilian. There were even texts written in Occitan, which was used by only a small number of people, although the latter wielded a disproportionately large influence on Navarrese society. Basque, the language of the majority of the population, was absolutely marginalised. The historian José María Lacarra (1957: 12) said of it:

> Of course, the notaries or "scribes" of the documents are aware that the people around them speak a language other than the Latin of their documents. This language will be described as "rustic," "vulgar," or "perverse," but they have to refer to it constantly to clarify the text. On many other occasions – on most occasions – they introduce toponyms or nicknames without feeling obliged to make the slightest comment, but one gets the impression from reading these documents that their meaning was intelligible to all.[5]

The presence of Castilian probably became more evident starting in 1492, when the Kingdom of Castile began to take control of the immense American market. Many Basques took an active part in this enterprise, and many chose to leave the Basque Country and seek work abroad. Learning Castilian became an absolute necessity, while the use of Basque was relegated to a lower level. The Bizkaian calligrapher Pedro Madariaga reflected as follows in his book *Honra de escribanos* (Honour of scribes), published in 1565 (Urkijo 1922 [1969]: 250):

> I cannot stop being angry with my Bizkaians for not using [the Basque language] in letters and business; and this leads many people to think that they cannot write, although there are books printed in this language.[6]

The description of the state of the language in Gasteiz by the Italian traveller Giovanni Battista Venturino in 1572 confirms that simple people spoke Basque whereas the nobility used "clear" Castilian (Santoyo 1972: 54):

> It seems that in [Gasteiz] the townspeople speak Bizkaian or Basque, as they call it, a language extremely hard to learn, although the nobles speak Castilian with utmost clarity.[7]

Eloquent too is the way in which Basque is pictured in the comedy *La toquera vizcaina* (The Basque woman head-dress seller). In this work by Pérez de Montalván, published in 1636, a dialogue ensues between Doña Elena and Caballero Lisandro (Pérez de Montalván 1636: 185):

> Lisandro: How, being Bizkaian, do you speak our language so well?
> Elena: Because it is less used in Bizkaia, and among the nobles it is considered less valuable to speak Basque, and better to speak fine Castilian. [8]

The first bans on the use of Basque date from the sixteenth century, in political bodies in Gipuzkoa, Araba, and Bizkaia. Notices of prohibition were repeated in following years, indicating that the population was mostly Basque-speaking. In many places, it was hard to find representatives who knew Castilian. This is clear, for example, from the agreement made public by the Juntas Generales of Araba in 1682 (Knörr 1994: 2):

> In this Junta, recognising that the procurator who came on behalf of the *Hermandad* of Artziniega did not know Romance, and did not understand what the said gentlemen resolved and decreed, it was considered, given that the inconvenience caused by his lack of understanding originated with his *Hermandad*, that he cannot speak and vote on the business treated in this said Junta. They decreed that henceforth the procurators from each *Hermandad* must be people most suitable and capable so that they can vote safely and appear in all available cases in the Juntas, and that if they fail to do so, the *Hermandad* that sends them will be fined five thousand maravedís, and the procurator that does not know Romance will be fined another five thousand maravedís. [...] Don Antonio Gonzalez de Zuazo y Mújica, procurator of the *Hermandad* of Aramayona, protested against the said decree, but the said gentlemen nevertheless ordered that it be executed thenceforth, and that in addition procurators that did not know Romance would be thrown out of the Junta.[9]

In the mid-eighteenth century, the Jesuit Manuel Larramendi described the state of Basque in Gipuzkoa as follows (Larramendi 1745: CLXIII):

> Here Castilian is quite common, especially in the bigger places, among the ecclesiastics, the nobility, and other cultivated persons. Here people frequently speak and preach in Castilian, and the sermons preached in the Juntas Generales in the province [Gipuzkoa] are in the same language. Here people speak and write in Castilian, and hardly anything is ever written in Basque. Here people learn to read and write in Castilian, and they even forbid the children to speak Basque, although without any foundation. Here deeds, agreements, and public contracts are done in Castilian. Here court hearings and the like are enacted and dispatched in Castilian. Here the *corregidores* (local administrative and judicial officials), the captains, the intendants, and other ministers of the king speak, govern, and give their orders in Castilian. Even the *fueros* of the province and the particular ordinances of the towns are in Castilian. Provincials [Gipuzkoans], Bizkaians, Arabans, and Navarrese have printed and continue to print books in Castilian.[10]

As I have already mentioned, starting in the eighteenth century, as a result of the decree of Nueva Planta (in 1716), the Spanish state implemented a policy directly aimed at marginalising all languages other than Castilian.

Basque in the north of the Basque Country

Up to now I have talked mainly about the linguistic situation in the southern Basque provinces (within the Spanish state). Things were not much different in the north (in the French state), but some special nuances deserve attention. The Protestant Reformation and the Counter-Reformation that followed had much to do with them.

Like the rest of France, France's Basque provinces were immersed in the so-called "wars of religion." The promoters of Protestantism made use of national languages, thus departing from the practice followed up until then by the Catholic Church, which had exclusively used Latin, the "ecumenical" language, throughout Western Europe. It is enough to remember that the Queen of Béarn and Lower Navarre, Joana of Albret, converted in 1559 to Calvinist Protestantism and had the New Testament translated into Basque, a task that was carried out by the priest Joanes Leizarraga in 1571, with the help of four others (Leizarraga 1571). Three individuals remained for a year under the tutelage of Leizarraga, in order to perfect their study of Basque, which suggests that the language, at least in daily life, enjoyed a great vitality (Lacombe 1931 [1972]: 365).

The Catholic Church was not insensitive to the new situation, and a group of ecclesiastics on the Lapurdian coast, acting as a team, strove to educate the population in the principles of Catholicism. They wrote and published a large number of works, notably including one titled *Guero* (Later), by the priest Pedro Agerre, better known as Axular, which appeared in 1643 (Axular 1643).

Some of these books were reprinted, which suggests that a large number of people were able to read and understand them. A course in Basque, titled *L'interprect ou Traduction du François, Espagnol et Basque*, had numerous reprints. It was composed by Voltoire around 1620 and based on the speech of the Lapurdian coast, which shows that Basque was habitually used in commercial activities in the area, mainly around the fishing ports of Ziburu (Ciboure) and Donibane Lohizune (Saint-Jean-de-Luz). It is well known that two churchmen came from France to perform pastoral work in Lapurdi, Esteve Materra, and Sylvain Pouvreau, and that they learned the language of the region and later used it to write books.

So things were somewhat different in the northern Basque Country to the way they were in regions south of the Pyrenees, where throughout the sixteenth and seventeenth centuries publications in Basque seem to have been only collections of proverbs, following the taste of the Renaissance, and a few catechisms and religious books of a very humble level, translated from Castilian on the express orders of the bishops, who thus fulfilled the dictates of the Council of Trent (1545–63) in matters of vernacular languages. There were a few other works, such as a vocabulary apparently created in Gasteiz in 1562, at the wish of the Italian Niccolò Landucci (or Nicholao Landuchio; Landucci 1562), and a Basque course translated from Castilian into the speech of the Bilbao region by the priest

Rafael Mikoleta in 1653 (Mikoleta 1653). All these works, however, came to light much later, or ended up being lost altogether – an indication of the scant interest that the educated classes had for Basque.

In the northern Basque Country too, the doors of the administration were closed to Basque. Occitan, or, to be more precise, its Gascon dialect, was the official language of Zuberoa and Lower Navarre. For example, the charters of Lapurdi (1514) and Zuberoa (1520), as well as a renewed edition of those of Lower Navarre (1611), were written in Gascon. Starting in 1539, following the publication of the Villers-Cotterêts decree, French was the only language that could be used in courts of law. In short, the language of culture was for a long time Latin while, as early as the seventeenth century, French came to be imposed. After the French Revolution of 1789 all languages other than French were definitively discarded from an official point of view (see Certeau, Julia, and Revel 1975 and Oyharçabal 2001).

In conclusion, Basque continued to be marginalised more or less uninterruptedly until the end of the twentieth century, while during the period of General Franco's dictatorship things got even worse: Basque was not only marginalised but banned and persecuted.

With the death of the dictator Franco, important changes came about in the Basque Autonomous Community (Araba, Bizkaia, and Gipuzkoa) and in the northwestern part of Navarre, where starting in 1979 Basque became an official language, alongside Castilian. However, in most of Navarre and in the three Basque provinces of the French state practically nothing changed.

The marginalisation of Basque in education

Here, I look specifically at education, for it has a particularly direct impact on dialectal fragmentation. It is in schools that the standard language is taught and, thanks to their activities, that the language preserves its unity and curbs its natural tendency to diverge.

As far as the southern provinces are concerned, Basque had no place at all in teaching until 1960, with the exception of some sporadic and unstable experiments. After the experience of the *ikastolak*, in 1979–80, Basque was gradually incorporated into the public-school system in the provinces of Araba, Bizkaia, and Gipuzkoa and in Navarre's so-called "Basque-speaking zone" and "mixed zone."

In the past, Basque was not merely marginalised but was systematically prohibited. Teachers routinely used a ring or some similar object to humiliate students caught speaking Basque. Anyone given the ring had to pass it on to whoever was caught next, and at the end of the day or week the student in possession of the ring was duly punished. This started from the very moment children began attending school, usually at the age of 6. This practice seems to have begun as a result of the Nueva Planta decree in 1716. The first mention of it so far discovered dates from 1745, in the prologue to the dictionary by Larramendi (1745: LII):

Even children at school learn to read and write in Castilian, and not at all in Basque, but it is wrong to forbid children to speak their mother tongue.[11]

Some years later, the Jesuit Agustín Kardaberatz (1761: 17) denounced the use of the ring and of physical punishment:

There has never been a language more miserable than Basque. They want to make it disappear and bury it underground, without taking into account that it is our mother tongue, as if speaking Basque were the greatest sin. They even want to ban it from schools, by using rings and signboards, whips and punishments.[12]

From then on, such complaints became constant and habitual (see, for example, Lasa 1968 and Garate 1972, 1976). Here, I will cite only one, that of Pablo Mendibil, born in Araba in the town of Dulantzi in 1788, who gives a first-person account of his experience (Garate 1972: 174):

Because my language is Basque, and in order to force me to forget it as if it were incompatible with learning and knowing Castilian, I am condemned to receive the cursed ring if I let slip a single word of the sort that I sucked in with my mother's milk, even though I say *ama* instead of *madre* (mother) or *Jaungoicoa* instead of *Dios* (God), in my attempt to invoke God's holy name. The ring of my sins is found to be in my possession. A crime worse than *lèse* magisterial authority! [...] And what if the ring fails to appear? What if, to avoid this happening, one hides the ring or shatters it into pieces and no one produces it? In that case, woe betide the last one to have had it! He is held to account. And if no one had it and no one gave it to the master? All will be whipped. And who gets it on the shoulders? The ones who have been singled out. And who carries out the sentence? Four or five classmates, chosen from among the most robust and malicious, who are considered to be untouchable, solely because they act as executioners, pounce like dogs of prey on the unfortunate victim, spanking him and dragging him before the master's chair, pulling his clothes off and putting him in range so that he cannot escape the disciplinary blows.[13]

The punishments handed out at school were complemented in many cases by obligations imposed on pupils' parents by the teachers. In the Navarrese valley of Burunda, in the autumn of 2007, during my fieldwork, an elderly lady told me that one of her granddaughters spoke exclusively in Castilian, while the rest of the family always spoke in Basque. Apparently, the child's teacher had told her parents that she was a slow learner, and this was because of her lack of mastery of Castilian, so they would do better in future to speak Castilian with her, a suggestion that the grandmother followed to the letter.

This attitude was standard and commonplace throughout the Basque Country.

Things were somewhat different in the northern Basque provinces. As Beñat Oyharçabal (1999) has pointed out, in France most low-income families sent their children to the so-called *petites écoles* (small schools), which existed until the nineteenth century. At first, they were controlled by the municipality. In 1698, they passed into the hands of the royal authority, but the Church played an important role in them. Essentially, they taught Christian doctrine and reading and writing, all done in Basque.

The children of wealthy families received instruction in Latin and, as early as the seventeenth century, in French. However, the ring was also used in France, at latest starting in the nineteenth century.

Some consequences of the marginalisation of Basque

When a language is marginalised in society, its speakers end up thinking that it is worthless and useless. This perception is further aggravated when its speakers are forced to emigrate, as has been the case throughout the Basque Country over many centuries. Learning the language of the place to which you migrate becomes a pressing need, while your own language begins to matter less. In the case of the southern Basque provinces, it is also necessary to take into account the negative effect of the defeats suffered in the Carlist wars (1833–39 and 1872–76) and, above all, in 1936, at the hands of Franco. Most of the important public offices (teachers, senior local officials, sometimes even priests) were filled by people attached to the regime and who usually came from outside the Basque Country.

People who suffer in this way seldom make their views public, let alone in writing, but some relevant testimony has fortunately been preserved. Here is a letter written to his mother by the Dominican friar Balentin Berrio-Otxoa, martyred in 1861 in Tonkin, where he was a missionary, and canonised in 1988. The letter was probably written in 1859. It says (Berrio-Otxoa 2006 [Berriozabal, ed.]: 112):

> Mother, when we meet in Heaven we will have to speak in Castilian, because Basque has almost been forgotten.[14] Speak Castilian there, Mother; you cannot speak Basque there, so you need to learn Castilian from the soldiers. You, Mother, are now old, it is hard to learn Castilian, I believe, and will cause you much headache; but if you do not learn it now, later you will not be able to speak with your son in Heaven.[15]

Throughout the twentieth century, some Basque intellectuals, notably Miguel Unamuno (1864–1936), a Bilbaoan, and professor and rector at the University of Salamanca, who was highly regarded in Spain in his time, expressed similar opinions. Here are some extracts from his opening speech at the Floral Games in Bilbao in 1901 (Unamuno 1901 [1958]):

For many peoples, as for other organisms, there are times of change. We are in such a time. Millenarian Basque has no room for modern thinking; in Bilbao, speaking Basque, is a nonsense. [...] We have to forget it and burst into Castilian (pp. 298–9).

Our soul is greater than its ancient dress; Basque is already narrow; and since its material and fabric do not lend themselves to widening, let us break with it. There is, moreover, a law of economics, that it costs us less effort to learn Castilian than to transform Basque, which is a superfluous and complicated instrument far from the simplicity and sobriety of means of analytical languages. And do not say that it would not be our thinking, truly ours, if expressed in a language other than our own (pp. 299–300).

And Basque? [...] Let us bury it in all holiness, with dignified funeral rites, embalmed in science; let us bequeath to study this most interesting relic (p. 300).[16]

In his essay *The Life of Don Quixote and Sancho*, Unamuno warned of the need to dismount from the "stubborn mule," that is, to abandon Basque (Unamuno 1905: 125):

Learn, at the same time, to embody your thinking in a language of culture, leaving behind the millenarian language of our parents; dismount from the mule, and our spirit, the spirit of our caste, will circle the entire world in that language, in the language of Don Quixote, just as the caravel of our Sebastián Elcano, the strong son of Getaria, circled for the first time around the world.[17]

A fragment of dialogue between various characters in Unamuno's novel *Niebla* (Fog; Unamuno 1914: 833) contains a possible clue to Unamuno's views on the plurilingual nature of the Spanish state:

"But do not you think, Madame," asked Augusto, "that it would be good if there were only one language?"

"Exactly!" exclaimed Don Fermín.

"Indeed I do, sir," said the aunt, staunchly; "a single language: Castilian, as well as, at most, a dialect in which to talk to the maids, who are not rational."[18]

Changes in the structure of Basque

Given its inferior status in relation to the other languages with which it has been in contact, Basque has usually been more accustomed to receiving than to giving. It is true that some Basque words have passed into other languages, such as *ezkerra* (left), which has become *izquierda* in Castilian. Some have even become part of a wider international vocabulary. This is the case, for example, with words like *akelarre* (witches' Sabbath), *jai alai* (a variation of Basque pelota), and *silueta* (silhouette), from the surname of a French government minister of Basque origin. But they are exceptions: most loans have come in the opposite direction.

Naturally, Basque has been enriched by its many foreign loans. From Latin, for example, it has adopted a large number of words relating to religion. Such is the case with *abendu* (December, advent), *aingeru* (angel), *arima* (soul), *barkatu* (pardon), *bataio* (baptism), *bedeinkatu* (blessed), *bekatu* (sin), *birjina* (virgin), *borondate* (will), *deabru* (devil), *eliza* (church), *fede* (faith), *garizuma* (Lent), *gurutze* (cross), *infernu* (hell), *meza* (mass), and *zeru* (heaven, firmament), which have been perfectly assimilated into all the Basque dialects.

But not everything has been equally beneficial and enriching. There has also been much loss and deterioration. The period since 1960 is a good example. A great effort has been made to train new Basque speakers and to instruct in the new standard language those who already know Basque. In general, the campaign has been successful, especially quantitatively. Qualitatively, however, deep cracks have begun to appear in the structure of the language. I am referring not to the Basque spoken by those who have learned it from scratch but to that used by young generations of native speakers. People are insufficiently aware of this problem, and do not always take the necessary measures to remedy it.

To give an example, those teaching Basque rarely pay much attention to its phonological system – the accent or the pronunciation of certain phonemes specific to the language. As a result, the phonological system of Basque is beginning to deteriorate. It is losing some of its essential features and assimilating to French or Castilian. Examples include the pronunciation of the sibilant consonants (*s, x, z, ts, tx, tz*) in several regions and of the vibrants (*r* and *rr*) in the northern provinces and the loss of aspiration and of the palatals *dd* and *tt*, which are disappearing because they have no equivalent in the dominant language.

Every language is subject to constant change, to which it must be able to adapt, but in the case of languages like Basque, which have to compete, in the same space, with other more important and better protected languages, not all change is good. It is necessary to put barriers in the way of the dominant languages. Otherwise, minority and marginalised languages will dissolve into the majority hegemonic ones.

The dialectal diversification of Basque

My reflections on the Basque dialects will be a central theme of this study, but here I anticipate one of my main concerns – the high degree of fragmentation of the language. The first in-depth study of the Basque dialects was made by Louis-Lucien Bonaparte (1813–1891), a relative of the Emperor, who devoted many years of his life to this work, and who, despite living in London, seems to have achieved an acceptable level of practical mastery of Basque.

According to the classification Bonaparte made in the years 1863–69 (Bonaparte 1863, 1869), and to which he returned in later years, there were eight Basque dialects, twenty-five subdialects, and thirty-six minor varieties. The classification was as follows: Bizkaian, with three subdialects and nine varieties; Gipuzkoan, with three subdialects and five varieties; northern Upper Navarrese, with six subdialects; southern Upper Navarrese, with three subdialects and eight varieties; Lapurdian, with two subdialects and three varieties; western Lower Navarrese, with three subdialects and two varieties; eastern Lower Navarrese, with three subdialects and six varieties; and Zuberoan, with two subdialects and three varieties.

Bonaparte (1869: 226 and 424) recognised, however, that the dialects could also number between six and nine, if different criteria were applied. For example, the two Upper Navarrese and the two Lower Navarrese dialects, a total of four, could be reduced to just two, while the dialect of the Navarrese Erronkari Valley [Roncal in Spanish] could be considered a true dialect, distinct from Zuberoan. I consider, like the lexicographer Resurrección María Azkue (1905: xxvi–xxvii), that Bonaparte's classification is improved by these corrections, and that it would also be a good idea to reduce the number of subdialects and varieties.

In the years since the mid-nineteenth century, four important changes have taken place.

1   Basque has suffered a considerable decline. The speech communities of the Navarrese valleys of Zaraitzu [Salazar in Spanish] and Erronkari, for example, which, though different one from the other, were similar in structure and formed a separate dialect, have disappeared completely.
2   Since 1960, dialects have tended to converge, due to the fact that Basque was introduced into the official education system, a standard language was created, and gradually the language began to make headway in places from which it had previously been excluded. As a result, dialectal diversification is now less extensive than it was at the time of Bonaparte.
3   Standard Basque has emerged, using the Gipuzkoan dialect as its base. As a consequence, surrounding speech communities, especially to the west and in Navarre, have tended to assimilate and even to merge with it.
4   Basque studies have taken off during the last few decades. The creation of Departments of Basque Philology in the universities was decisive in this respect. Thanks to this development, today we know incomparably more about the language than in Bonaparte's time.

Today, there are, in my opinion, five Basque dialects, ten subdialects, and 17 minor varieties (Zuazo 2013, 2014). They are as follows:

1   *Western dialect*, which includes the Basque-speaking parts of Bizkaia province, much of the Gipuzkoan valley of Deba, and Aramaio (Aramayona) in the province of Araba. It has two subdialects and seven varieties.
2   *Central dialect*, spoken in the greater part of Gipuzkoa and the western part of Navarre. It has two subdialects and six varieties.

3   *Navarrese dialect*, spoken in most Basque-speaking parts of the province of Navarre. It has four subdialects and three varieties.
4   *Navarrese-Lapurdian dialect*, spoken in the provinces of Lapurdi and Lower Navarre, in some places in northwestern Zuberoa, and in the Navarrese valley of Luzaide (Valcarlos). It has two subdialects and one variety.
5   *Zuberoan dialect*, spoken in most of Zuberoa and in Eskiula in Béarn. It is a very homogeneous dialect with no subdialects or varieties sufficiently distinct to count separately.

Factors that explain the survival of Basque

Given its tortured past, it may seem remarkable that Basque continues to survive. Everything has seemed to militate against it: it has relatively few speakers, powerful nearby rivals, and a seeming incapacity to face up to its adversaries. But in that case, what can account for its endurance into the twenty-first century?

Basque's essential features

The language has clearly played, and continues to play, a fundamental role in forming the Basque character. It is enough to recall the name by which Basques have called their country, ever since the first documents were written, in

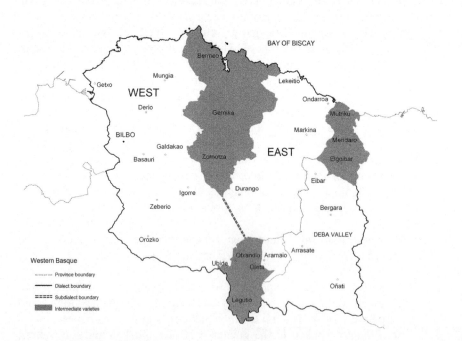

Figure 1.1 Western Basque

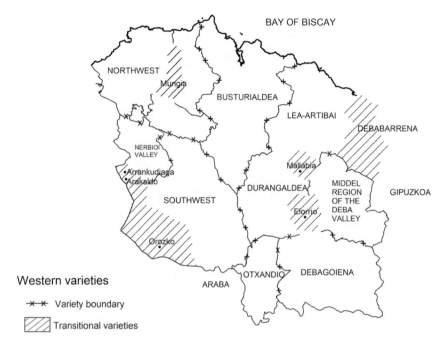

Figure 1.2 Western varieties

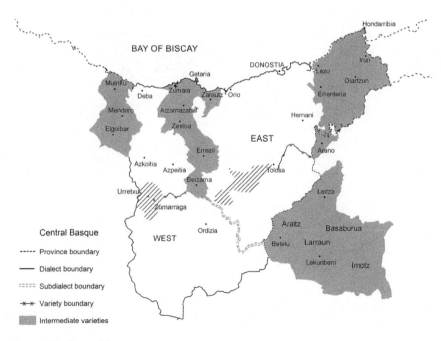

Figure 1.3 Central Basque

Figure 1.4 Navarrese Basque

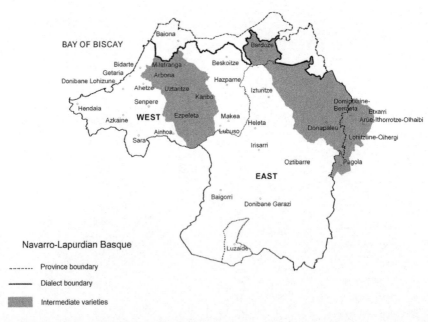

Figure 1.5 Navarro-Lapurdian Basque

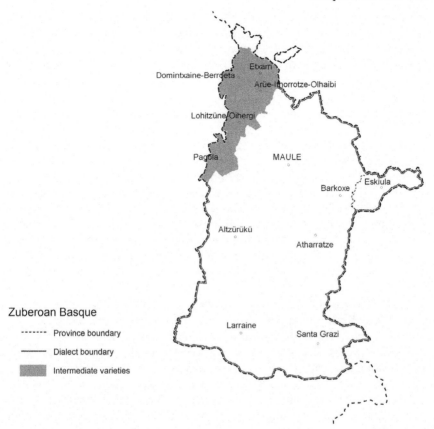

Zuberoan Basque

------- Province boundary

——— Dialect boundary

▓ Intermediate varieties

Figure 1.6 Zuberoan Basque

the sixteenth century: *Euskal Herria*, which comes from *Euskararen Herria*, "the country of Basque." The word *euskaldun* has been used to refer to those "who speak Basque," whereas *erdaldun* is used to designate "those who speak another language." Victor Hugo (1802–1885) was not exaggerating when he said, in the course of a visit to the Basque Country in 1843 (Aren 2002: 62):

> Singular and, undoubtedly, worthy of study. I would add that a deep and secret link, which nothing has been able to undo, unites all members of the mysterious Basque family, despite the treaties, these diplomatic frontiers, and even despite the Pyrenees, these natural frontiers. [...] One is born Basque, one speaks Basque, one lives as a Basque, and one dies as a Basque. The Basque language is a fatherland, I would almost say a religion. Say a Basque word to a montagnard: up until that word, you were hardly a man for him; then you are his brother.[19]

Unsurprisingly, at certain times in history there have been attempts to alter and weaken this way of thinking. During the Carlist wars, in the nineteenth century, the Basque clergy, who were mostly Carlist, equated religion and *fueros* with the use of the Basque language. Hence the well-known slogan *euskaldun = fededun*, meaning Basque = (Catholic) believer. This idea was expressed in the following passage from a work by José Ignacio Arana (1838–1896), a Jesuit closely linked to the Carlist side (Arana 1872: 205–6):

> The eternal happiness of the Basque Country depends upon the following three pillars: the *Christian faith*, together with the healthy customs on which Christianity is founded; its own self-government and its own *fueros*; and its ancient and beautiful *language*. It is precisely these three principles that those who wish to destroy and sink the Basque Country tirelessly seek to undermine. It is therefore essential to confront them and to deal with them energetically if prudently. This is one of the main reasons for maintaining, protecting, and extolling Basque.[20]

After the defeat in the Second Carlist War (1876), the *fueros*, which formed the basis for self-government, were completely abolished. Their abolition coincided with the start of industrialisation, which drew in a veritable wave of immigrants from various Spanish regions. These immigrants settled mainly in the mining area around Bilbao. It was in this context, in 1895, that the Basque Nationalist Party was born, in Bilbao. It was strongly xenophobic in character in its first years. Ethnicity rather than language animated this incipient nationalism (see, for example, Arana Goiri 1894 [1980]: 404). It is therefore not surprising that Sabino Arana Goiri sought to change the traditional name *Euskal Herria*, "the country of Basque," to a name of his own coining, in which the concept of Basque ethnicity predominated: *Euzkadi*, "land of the Euzkos."[21]

The support of the Church

The Catholic Church has been one of the few institutions, if not the only one, to have supported Basque. However, not all parts of the Church promoted the Basque language, nor did support for Basque exist at all times and in all parts of the Basque Country.

Support for Basque came from the priests and the members of certain congregations of friars (not including nuns), among them Benedictines, Capuchins, Carmelites, Franciscans, Jesuits, and Passionists. I have already mentioned the important role played by such people in the northern provinces during the Counter-Reformation in the seventeenth century and during the Calvinist Reformation in the previous century.

During the French Revolution too, the Church played a prominent role in defending the historical rights of the Basque Country, including the Basque language, although other factors proper to the Church itself and that had nothing to do with the Basques and their language also intervened. The Barère Report said in this regard (Certeau, Julia and Revel 1975: 294):

> I want to talk about the Basque people. They occupy the extreme western part of the Pyrenees, next to the ocean. Their sonorous and luminous language is considered as the emblem of their origin and of the heritage transmitted by their ancestors. But they have priests, and the priests use their language to make the people fanatical, and they are ignorant of the French language and the language of the laws of the Republic.[22]

In the southern provinces the Church has also played a prominent role in defending the language, but only from the eighteenth century onwards, and those who did so were mainly Jesuits and Franciscans. The Jesuit professor of the University of Salamanca, Manuel Larramendi, was very explicit in this regard. In his work *Corografía de Gipuzkoa*,[23] written in the mid-eighteenth century but not published until the twentieth, he presented a rich picture of the behavior of the clergy (Larramendi 1969):

> Those who should be best versed [in the use of the Basque language] are in fact least versed in it and speak Basque without a shred of dignity and intelligence. These are the ecclesiastics, religious people, gentlefolk, and people accustomed since childhood to Castilian or to the grammar they learned from Latin (p. 283).
>
> This enemy is he who suggests excuses of this nature, so that preachers, confessors, churchmen and non-churchmen, and Basques can go to sleep as far as Basque is concerned and live happily with the Castilian they know (p. 285).
>
> And there is even the disgrace of using these preachers to create a situation such that in many towns, communities of nuns, and brotherhoods, someone who preaches in Basque is less esteemed, since Basque is only the language of villagers, tenants, and poor people: a more damaging piece of deviltry has never entered the pulpits (p. 287).[24]

But he also warned:

> There can be no doubt that over the past few years in these parts sermons in Basque are not as bad as they were in the past, and that there are preachers who in moral sermons preach very well and lucidly, and to the taste and edification of their listeners. This is true of most of the missionaries in their sermons, and especially the Franciscan missionaries of Zarautz [p. 291].[25]

Some reflections on the future

The number of Basque speakers

As we have seen, since the 1960s the tendency towards a decline of the language has slowed, and there has been a notable increase in the number of Basque speakers, of whom there are now some 860,000. But this means that if the total population of the Basque Country exceeds three million, more than two million either know no Basque or do not know enough to express themselves fluently and confidently in it.

The increase in the number of Basque speakers has happened mainly in the three provinces that make up the Basque Autonomous Community: Araba, Bizkaia, and Gipuzkoa. In Navarre and in the three Basque regions of the French state, there have been no substantial changes. Needless to say, all this constitutes a serious obstacle to the normalisation of the use of Basque.

Attitudes towards Basque

Within the ambit of the Basque Autonomous Community and the western part of Navarre, among people born after the 1970s, the age-old stigma of Basque as a poor language, spoken by uneducated people, rural in character, and unserviceable for modern life has been overcome. This is a hugely positive step towards normalising the language. Again, however, we must not forget that in many parts of Navarre and in the northern regions, even in the minds of Basque speakers themselves, Basque continues to have the stigma of a rural language, a mode of expression associated with people of a low economic and cultural level. It is also frequently associated with radical nationalist ideologies.

On the other hand, one cannot but value highly the existence of an important group of people who, having arrived in the Basque Country from other places or having been born there to immigrant families, have learned Basque. Many have done so enthusiastically, often overcoming major difficulties. Many have achieved a complete mastery of the language, on a par with that of native speakers. Undoubtedly, this has had an enormously positive effect on efforts to normalise the language.

The quality of the language

I have already mentioned that the structure of Basque has undergone profound changes over the last few decades, because of its dependent status in relation to French and Castilian. This is an undeniable fact, but it is also true that large numbers of people use the language correctly. If we take the state of Basque literature as an indicator, we can rest assured that there are today more Basque writers than in the entire history of the Basque Country, and that the quality of the language used in their writing is unprecedentedly high.

This suggests that the normalisation of the language is likely to proceed apace.

The dialect division of Basque

The fact that Basque, which occupies a relatively small territorial base, is divided into so many dialects is highly relevant to the issues raised in this chapter. Basque has been transmitted orally over the centuries, it has been marginalised in administration and schooling, and it has barely been used in writing. That the Basque speech community is divided between the French and Spanish states, and that French and Spanish have been the only official languages for centuries, has also increased the degree of separation between the dialects spoken on either side of the Franco-Spanish border. Now that a standard language exists and Basque has entered domains from which it was previously shut out, the distance between dialects has shortened. This too will greatly profit the campaign to normalise the language.

Notes

1 El alcalde de Oia-Castro mandó prendar don Morial, que era Merino de Castilla, porque juzgara que el ome de Oia-Castro si le demandase ome de fuera de la villa o de la villa, que el recudiese en bascuence. Et de si sopo don Morial en verdad, que tal fuero habían los de Oia-Castro.
2 Item nuyl corredor nonsia usado que faga mercaderia ninguna, que compre nin venda entre ningunas personas, faulando en algaravia ni en abraych ni en basquenç: et qui lo fara pague por coto xxx sol.
3 Los navegantes de la provincia de Guipúzcoa y señorío de Vizcaya, y tierra de vascos, yendo cada año una vez a Terranova a la pesquería de los bacalaos y ballenas, vienen a [a]prender esta lengua los salvajes de aquella región, con harta poca comunicación de tiempo breve, que con las gentes de aquí tienen una vez al año, en espacio de menos de dos meses.
4 Alegaron que toda la vida, antes incluso de que se conocieran esos lugares, los vascos ya traficaban allí, hasta el punto que los canadienses no negocian con los franceses en otra lengua que la de los vascos.
5 Desde luego, los notarios o "escribas" de los documentos tienen conciencia de que las gentes que les rodean hablan una lengua distinta del latín de sus documentos. Esta lengua será calificada de "rústica", de "vulgar", de "sórdida", pero tienen que referirse a ella constantemente para aclarar el texto. Otras muchas veces –las más– introducen topónimos o apodos sin creerse obligados a hacer advertencia alguna, pero de su lectura sacamos la impresión de que su significado era inteligible a todos.
6 Yo no puedo dexar de tomar un poco de cólera con mis vizcaínos porque no se sirven de ella en cartas y negocios; y dan ocasión a muchos de pensar que no se puede escribir, habiendo libros impresos en esta lengua.
7 E Vittoria capo di Alava, vicina à Vipusca et à Biscaglia, (...) et si vede che le persone plebee in essa parlano Biscaino ò Bascongado come dicono, che é difficilliss[im]a lingua d'apprendere, se bene li nobili parlano chiaramente Castigliano.
8 Lisandro: ¿Cómo siendo vizcaína hablas tan bien nuestra lengua?
   Elena: Porque es en Vizcaya mengua, y entre los nobles mohína, hablar vasquençe jamás, sino fino castellano.

9   En esta Junta, habiendo reconocido que el procurador que vino por la Hermandad de Arciniega no sabía romance, ni entendía lo que dichos señores resolvían y decreta[ban], consideraron los inconvenientes que de no entender se pueden originar a su Hermandad, pues no se puede dar su voz y voto a los negocios que se tratan en esta dicha Junta. Decretaron que de aquí en adelante los procuradores que vinieren de cada Hermandad sean personas de las más idóneas y capaces para que puedan dar su sano voto y parecer en todos los casos que se puedan ofrecer en sus Juntas, y que si así no lo hicieren sea multada la Hermandad que le enviare en cinco mil maravedís, y el procurador que viniere que no supiere romance en otros cinco mil maravedís (...). Don Antonio González de Zuazo y Mújica, procurador de la Hermandad de Aramayona, protestó el dicho decreto, y dichos señores, sin embargo de dicha protesta, mandaron se ejecute de aquí adelante, y demás de dicha pena sean echados de la Junta los procuradores que vinieren y no supieren romance.

10 Aquí es corriente el castellano bastantemente, especialmente en los lugares mayores, entre todos los eclesiásticos, entre todos los caballeros, y otras personas cultivadas. Aquí se habla y se predica con frecuencia en castellano, y los sermones que se predican a las Juntas Generales de la provincia son en la misma lengua. Aquí se habla y se escribe en castellano, y apenas se escribe nada en bascuence. Aquí se aprende a leer y escribir en castellano, y aun se les prohíbe, aunque sin fundamento alguno, a los niños el hablar bascuence. Aquí las escrituras, y tratos, y contratos públicos se hacen en castellano. Aquí la Audiencia y todo se actúa y despacha en castellano. Aquí vienen los señores corregidores, aquí los capitanes generales, aquí los intendentes y otros ministros del rey, y hablan, y gobiernan, y dan sus órdenes en castellano. Aun los fueros de toda la provincia, y las ordenanzas particulares de los pueblos están en castellano. Provincianos, bizcainos, alabeses y navarros han impreso e imprimen libros en castellano.

11 Hasta en las escuelas de niños se aprende a leer y escribir en castellano, y nada en bascuence, y aun con errada conducta se prohibe a los muchachos hablar su lengua materna.

12 Gendeen artean beste lenguageric eusquera baño dicha gabeagoric ezta icusi, ta gure jatorrizco edo jaiotzaco izquera ezbaliz bezala, ta euscaraz itzeguitea pecaturic aundiena baliz bezala, guiza artetic quendu ta lurpean ondatu nai dute, ta escoletan sortija edo siñaleaquin, azote ta castiguaquin eragotci nai dute.

13 Que mi lengua es la bascongada, y para obligarme a que la olvide como si fuera incompatible con aprender y saber la castellana, me condenan a recibir el maldito anillo si se me escapa una sola palabra de las que mamé con la leche, aunque diga *ama* en lugar de *madre,* o pronuncie *Jaungoicoa* en lugar de *Dios,* queriendo invocar su santo nombre. El anillo de mis pecados acierta a hallarse en mi poder. ¡Crimen peor que de lesa autoridad magisterial! (...) ¿Y si no aparece el anillo? ¿Si para evitar ese paso se oculta o de una vez se hace pedazos y nadie lo saca? En tal caso ¡ay del último que lo tuvo! Él es responsable ¿Y si nadie lo tuvo y lo dio el señor maestro? Todos serán azotados. ¡Cómo todos! ¿Y quién los toma a cuestas? Los señalados ¿Qué funcionarios son ésos? Cuatro o seis condiscípulos, escogidos entre los más robustos y malintencionados, que son tenidos por intangibles, sólo porque hacen oficio de verdugos para arrojarse como perros de presa sobre el infeliz condenado a azotaina, sujetarle, desembragarle y llevarle delante de la poltrona del señor maestro, poniéndolo descubierto y bien a tiro para que no yerre el golpe de la crujiente disciplina.

14 This first sentence, like most of the rest of the letter, is in Basque: "Amacho, alcar ceruan icusten garianian, erdera berba eguin biarco dogu, zergaitic eusqueria ya astu da."

15 Allí hablar castellano, Madre; no puede vascuence, y así con soldados aprender castellano es necesario. Usted, Madre, ahora vieja, difícil aprender castellano, yo

creer, y mucho doler cabeza; pero ahora no aprender, y despúes el Madre hablar no puede a la hijo en el cielo.

16 Hay para muchos pueblos, como para otros organismos, épocas de muda. En ella estamos. En el milenario eusquera no cabe el pensamiento moderno; Bilbao, hablando vascuence, es un contrasentido. (...) Tenemos que olvidarlo e irrumpir en el castellano.

Nuestra alma es más grande ya que su vestido secular; el vascuence nos viene ya estrecho; y como su material y tejido no se prestan a ensancharse, rompámosle. Hay, además, una ley de economía, y es que nos cuesta menos esfuerzo aprender el castellano que transformar el vascuence, que es un instrumento sobrado complicado y muy lejos de la sencillez y sobriedad de medios de los idiomas analíticos. Y no digáis que no será nuestro pensamiento, verdaderamente nuestro, si en lengua que no sea la nuestra lo expresamos.

¿Y el vascuence? (...) Enterrémosle santamente, con dignos funerales, embalsamado en ciencia; leguemos a los estudios tan interesante reliquia.

17 Aprended, a la vez, a encarnar vuestro pensamiento en una lengua de cultura, dejando la milenaria de nuestros padres; apeaos de la mula luego y nuestro espíritu, el espíritu de nuestra casta, circundará en esa lengua, en la de Don Quijote, los mundos todos, como circundó por primera vez al orbe la carabela de nuestro Sebastián Elcano, el fuerte hijo de Guetaria, hijo de nuestro mar de Vizcaya.

18 –Pero ¿Vd. no cree, señora –le preguntó Augusto–, que sería bueno que no hubiese sino una sola lengua?

–¡Eso, eso! –exclamó alborozado don Fermín.

–Si, señor –dijo con firmeza la tía–; una sola lengua: el castellano, y a lo sumo el bable para hablar con las criadas que no son racionales.

19 Aspect singulier d'ailleurs et digne d'étude. J'ajoute qu'ici un lien secret et profond, et que rien n'a pu rompre, unit, même en dépit des traités, ces frontières diplomatiques, même en dépit des Pyrénées, ces frontières naturelles, tous les membres de la mystérieuse famille basque. (...) On naît basque, on parle basque, on vit basque et l'on meurt basque. La langue basque est une patrie, j'ai presque dit une religion. Dites un mot basque à un montagnard dans la montagne; avant ce mot, vous étiez à peine un homme pour lui; vous voilà son frère.

20 Euskalerriac beti illezcorra bere zorionean iraun dezan cimendutzat edo *iru arroca bici* ta pillare gogor becela daduzcanac dirade, *prestutasun cristauzcoa* cristauai dagozten oitura ederrakin, bere eraenmodu ta *bicilegue berekiac*, eta *bere izkera* eder millaca urtecoa; eta iru gauza oyen contra ai dira ta aico ere Euskalerria doacabetu, gaistotu ta ondamendi izugarrian amilduacitzeco aztalca bician dabiltzan eta diarduten etsai, arerio, eta naaspillazaleac. Beragatic gogor eguin bear zaye; eta contuz ibilli. Eta orra arrazoy portizenecoa-or euskera gordetzeco, escudatzeco eta goitutzeco.

21 Arana formed the word *Euzko,* "Basque person," by regressive etymology from the root-word *Eusk-* (cf. Euskera, "Basque language"), substituting *z* for *s.* The *-di* element was a collective suffix used by Arana to create other neologisms.

22 Je veux parler du peuple basque. Il occupe l'extrémité des Pyrénées-Occidentales qui se jette dans l'Océan. Une langue sonore et imagée est regardée comme le sceau de leur origine et l'héritage transmis par leurs ancêtres. Mais ils ont des prêtres, et les prêtres se servent de leur idiome pour les fanatiser; mais ils ignorent la langue française et la langue des lois de la République.

23 A *corografía* is a description of facts or geographic phenomena special to a given region.

24 Los que debieran estar más instruidos en lo dicho, son los que están menos y los que hablan el vascuence indignamente y sin rastro de inteligencia. Estos son los eclesiásticos, religiosos, caballeros y gentes acostumbradas desde chicos al castellano o a la gramática que aprendieron del latín.

Este enemigo es el que sugiere tal excusa para que los predicadores, confesores, así eclesiásticos como regulares, vascongados, se duerman en cuanto al vascuence y vivan contentos con el castellano que saben.

Y aun ha llegado la infamia a valerse de estos predicadores para que en muchos pueblos, comunidades de monjas y cofradías, se tenga por cosa de menos valer el que se predique en vascuence, como que el vascuence es solamente lengua para aldeanos, caseros y gente pobre: diablura más perjudicial no ha podido introducirse en los púlpitos.

25 No se puede dudar que, de pocos años a esta parte, se predica en vascuence menos mal que antes, y que hay predicadores que en sermones morales predican absolutamente bien y con limpieza, y con gusto y fruto de los oyentes. Así por lo común los misioneros en sus sermones, y con especialidad los franciscanos misioneros de Zarauz.

References

Arana, José Ignacio. 1872. *San Ignacio Loyolacoaren bicitza laburtua euskaraz eta gaztelaniaz*. Bilbao: Larumbe anayen moldizteguia.

Arana Goiri, Sabino. 1894. "Errores catalanistas". Reprinted in *Obras Completas de Sabino Arana Goiri* (I): 401–409. Donostia: Sendoa, 1980.

Aren, Jean-Pierre (ed.). 2002. *Victor Hugo et le Pays Basque*. Donostia: Elkar.

Axular (Pedro Agerre). 1643. *Guero*. Bordeaux: G. Milanges.

Azkue, Resurrección M. 1905–1906. *Diccionario vasco-español-francés*. Reprinted in Bilbao: Real Academia de la Lengua Vasca, 1984.

Bakker, Peter. 1991. "La lengua de las tribus costeras es medio vasca. Un pidgin vasco y amerindio utilizado por europeos y nativos americanos en Norteamérica, h. 1540-h. 1640". *Anuario del Seminario de Filología Vasca "Julio de Urquijo"*, 25–2: 439–467. Donostia: Diputación Foral de Gipuzkoa.

Berrio-Otxoa, Balentin. 2006. *Neure amatxo maitia. Euskerazko gutunak*. (R. Berriozabal, ed.) Bilbao: Labayru Ikastegia and Bilbao Bizkaia Kutxa Fundazioa.

Bonaparte, Louis-Lucien. 1863. *Carte des sept provinces basques, montrant la délimitation actuelle de l'euscara*. London.

Bonaparte, Louis-Lucien. 1869. *Le verbe basque en tableaux, accompagné de notes grammaticales, selon les huit dialectes de l'euskara*. Reprinted in (J. A. Arana Martija, ed.) *Opera omnia vasconice* (I): 221–442. Bilbao: Real Academia de la Lengua Vasca, 1991.

Certeau, Michel, Dominique Julia and Jacques Revel. 1975. *Une politique de la langue. La Révolution française et les patois*. Paris: Éditions Gallimard.

Deen, Nicolaas G. H. 1937. *Glossaria duo Vasco-Islandica*. Reprinted in *Anuario del Seminario de Filología Vasca "Julio de Urquijo"*, 25–2: 321–426. Donostia: Diputación Foral de Gipuzkoa, 1991.

Garate, Justo. 1972. "El anillo escolar en la proscripción del euskera". *Boletín de la Real Sociedad Vascongada de los Amigos del País*, 28: 174. Donostia: Diputación Foral de Gipuzkoa.

Garate, Justo. 1976. "El anillo escolar en la proscripción del euskera". *Fontes Linguae Vasconum*, 8, nº 24, 367–387. Iruña: Institución Príncipe de Viana.

Gorrochategui, Joaquín. 1984. *Estudio sobre la onomástica indígena de Aquitania*. Bilbao: Universidad del País Vasco.

Gorrochategui, Joaquín. 1995. "The Basque Language and its neighbors in Antiquity". (J. I. Hualde, J. A. Lakarra and R. L. Trask, eds.) *Towards a History of the Basque Language*: 31–63. Amsterdam and Philadelphia: John Benjamins.

Irigarai, Ángel (A. Apat-Echebarne). 1974. *Una geografía diacrónica del euskara en Navarra*. Iruña: Ediciones y Libros.

Irizar, Pedro. 1973. "Los dialectos y variedades de la lengua vasca. Estudio lingüístico-demográfico". *Boletín de la Real Sociedad Vascongada de los Amigos del País*, 29: 3–78. Donostia: Diputación Foral de Gipuzkoa.

Kardaberatz, Agustín. 1761. *Eusqueraren berri onac*. Reprinted in *Obras completas de Agustín de Kardaberaz* (i): 153–170. Bilbao: La Gran Enciclopedia Vasca, 1973.

Knörr, Henrike. 1994. "La lengua vasca y las Juntas Generales de Álava". *Landazuri*, nº 3, 2.

Lacarra, José María. 1957. *Vasconia medieval. Historia y filología. Anejos del Anuario del Seminario de Filología Vasca "Julio de Urquijo"*, nº 2. Donostia: Diputación Foral de Gipuzkoa.

Lacombe, Georges. 1931. "De nouveau sur Liçarrague et ses collaborateurs". *Revista Internacional de Estudios Vascos*, 22: 363–366. Reprinted in Bilbao: *La Gran Enciclopedia Vasca*, 1972.

Lancre, Pierre. 1613. *Tratado de brujería vasca. Descripción de la inconstancia de los malos ángeles y demonios*. Translated by Elena Barberena. Tafalla: Txalaparta, 2004.

Landucci, Niccolò, 1562. *Dictionarium linguae cantabricae*. Reprinted in (H. Knörr and K. Zuazo, eds.) *El euskara alavés. Estudios y textos*: 201–465. Gasteiz: Parlamento Vasco, 1998.

Larramendi, Manuel. 1745. *Diccionario trilingüe del castellano, bascuence y latín*. Donostia: Bartolomé Riesgo y Montero.

Larramendi, Manuel. 1969. *Corografía o descripción general de la muy noble y muy leal provincia de Guipúzcoa*. (J. I. Tellechea Idigoras, ed.) Donostia: Sociedad Guipuzcoana de Ediciones y Publicaciones.

Lasa, José Ignacio (dir.). 1968. *Sobre la enseñanza primaria en el País Vasco*. Donostia: Auñamendi.

Leizarraga, Joanes. 1571. *Jesus Christ gure Jaunaren Testamendu Berria*. La Rochelle: Pierre Hautin. Facsímil: Donostia, Hordago, 1979.

Merino Urrutia, José J.Bautista. 1978. *La lengua vasca en La Rioja y Burgos*. Logroño: Servicio de Cultura de la Excma. Diputación Provincial de Logroño.

Mikoleta, Rafael. 1653. *Modo breve de aprender la lengua vizcayna*. Reprinted in (A. Zelaieta, ed.) Bilbao: AEK, 1995.

Oyharçabal, Beñat. 1999. "Euskarazko irakaskintzaren historia: ororen eskolen ondotik, frantses iraultzaren garaiko eskola liburuxka bat". *Lapurdum*, nº 4, 81–105. Baiona: Centre de Recherches Iker.

Oyharçabal, Beñat. 2001. "Zenbait gogoeta euskarak letra hizkuntza gisa izan duen bilakaeraz (xvii-xviii. mendeak)". *Litterae Vasconicae*, nº 8, 9–46. Bilbao: Labayru Ikastegia.

Pérez de Montalván, Juan. 1636. *La toquera vizcaina*. Valencia.

Santoyo, Julio-César. 1972. *Viajeros por Álava. (Siglos xv a xviii)*. Gasteiz: Caja de Ahorros Municipal de la Ciudad de Vitoria.

Unamuno, Miguel. 1901. "Discurso en los Juegos Florales celebrados en Bilbao el día 26 de agosto de 1901". Reprinted in *Obras Completas* (vi): 290–307. Madrid: Afrodisio Aguado, 1958.

Unamuno, Miguel. 1905. *Vida de Don Quijote y Sancho*. Reprinted in *Obras Completas* (iv): 8–384. Madrid: Afrodisio Aguado, 1958.

Unamuno, Miguel 1914. *Niebla*. Reprinted in *Obras Completas* (ii): 781–1000. Madrid: Afrodisio Aguado, 1958.

Urkijo, Julio. 1922. "Notas de Bibliografía Vasca". *Revista Internacional de Estudios Vascos*, 13: 248–251. Reprinted in Bilbao: La Gran Enciclopedia Vasca, 1969.

Voltoire. 1620 (?). *L'Interprect ou Traduction du François, Espagnol & Basque*. Reprinted in (J. A. Lakarra, ed.) *Anuario del Seminario de Filología Vasca "Julio de Urquijo"*, 31–1 (1997): 1–66 and 33–2 (1999): 493–568. Donostia: Diputación Foral de Gipuzkoa.

Zuazo, Koldo. 2013. *The Dialects of Basque*. [Translated by Aritz Branton] Reno, Nevada: Center for Basque Studies.

Zuazo, Koldo 2014. *Euskalkiak*. Donostia: Elkar.

Zubiaur, José Ramón. 1990. *Las ideas lingüísticas vascas en el s. xvi (Zaldibia, Garibay, Poza)*. Donostia: Cuadernos Universitarios, Sección Euskal Filologia, nº 6, E.U.T.G.- Mundaiz.

2 Origin of the dialects

There are two schools of thought about the origin of the Basque dialects. One, the most widely held, argues that the dialects are very old, and date back to the period before the arrival of the Romans. The other holds that the present dialects arose in the Middle Ages. The latter theory is less widespread, but it is supported by most professional linguists. Curiously, the main exceptions to this statement are usually to be found in the field of dialectology: Allières (1981: 112), Alvarez Enparantza and Aurrekoetxea (1987: 5), Pagola (1991: 77–86), Pagola (1992: 42–44), and Arejita, Manterola and Oar-Arteta (2007: 37–39).

The pre-Roman origin of the dialects

The proponents of the thesis

The first person to classify the Basque dialects was the Zuberoan historian Arnaut Oihenart (1592–1667). He related them to the ancient tribes, about whose existence geographers and historians of Roman times had written. According to Oihenart (1656 [1971]: 353), there were four dialects, just as there were four tribes: (1) that of the Aquitans, spoken in the northern provinces of Lapurdi, Lower Navarre, and Zuberoa; (2) that of the Vascons, in Navarre; (3) that of the Vardules, in Gipuzkoa and Araba; and (4) that of the Autrigones of Bizkaia.

Although Oihenart was himself a Zuberoan speaker, he classified the dialect of his province in the same group as that of Lapurdi and Lower Navarre. By the seventeenth century, Zuberoan was clearly differentiated from the rest of the dialects, and it would seem that it was his reluctance to give up his theory that led Oihenart to assert its affinity with the dialects of Lapurdi and Lower Navarre.

During the eighteenth and nineteenth centuries, this question was seemingly dropped, for from 1745 onwards, with Manuel Larramendi leading the way (Larramendi 1745), the origin of Basque and its dialects was located in the confusion of languages at the time of Babel.

In the twentieth century, a third element was added to the relationship between tribes and dialects, that of ecclesiastical dioceses. In an article,

Serapio Mujika (1914–17 [1969]: 192–193) said that the boundaries of the dioceses were similar to those of the tribes, and that modern dialects were reminiscent of that ancient unity. This thesis was later taken up by Julio Caro Baroja in two widely read books, *Los pueblos del norte de la Península Ibérica* ("The peoples of the north of the Iberian Peninsula"; Baroja 1943) and *Materiales para una historia de la lengua vasca en su relación con la latina* ("Materials for a history of the Basque language in its relation with Latin"; Baroja 1945). In this way, the idea that the Basque dialects were ancient, and that their boundaries coincided with the demarcations of the tribes and the ecclesiastical dioceses, was widely accepted.

The bases for the argument

The thesis about the coincidence of tribe, diocesis, and dialect is only borne out in the western area, that is, Bizkaia, Araba, and Gipuzkoa's Deba Valley, and, to all intents and purposes, nowhere else. A relatively uniform language was spoken in the western area, ecclesiastically part of the bishopric of Araba, which in the late eleventh century was integrated into that of Calahorra and was said to be populated by the Caristios rather than by the Autrigones, as Oihenart had erroneously asserted.

The Gipuzkoan areas around Oiartzun, Hondarribia, and Irun are also often cited in support of the thesis. However, although this area is supposed to have been populated by Vascons and has been considered to feature a form of Navarrese (although some would dispute this), ecclesiastically it belonged to the bishopric of Baiona and not that of Iruña.

The mismatches between tribe, diocesis, and dialect are even greater in other places, which is presumably why they are usually kept out of the argument. For example, Prince Bonaparte distinguished four dialects in the northern Basque Country. Some of us believe that this number is exaggerated, but whatever the case, everyone agrees that there are at least two dialects, Zuberoan and Navarrese-Lapurdian. But the northern territory was divided into three bishoprics (Baiona, Dax, and Oloron) and, according to historians, was occupied by a single tribe.

It is hard to believe that Lapurdi and Lower Navarre were divided between the bishops of Dax and Baiona on linguistic grounds. The regions of Amikuze (Mixe) and Oztibarre (Ostabat), and the communes of Landibarre (Lantabat) and Bidaxune (Bidache), all in Lower Navarre, were integrated into the bishopric of Dax. But the dialect spoken in Oztibarre, part of the bishopric of Dax, differs hardly at all from that of the region of Garazi (Cize), part of the bishopric of Baiona.

Nor is the tribe–diocesis–dialect thesis borne out in Gipuzkoa and Navarre. Ecclesiastically, the greater part of these two provinces was contained within a single bishopric, that of Iruña. Even so, the above-mentioned authors affirm that they were populated by two different tribes, the

Vascons and the Vardulos and, from a linguistic point of view, spoke two main dialects, central and Navarrese – all the time forgetting the special speech forms of the Navarrese valleys of Zaraitzu and Erronkari.

Even if we reduce the scope of our investigation, the posited relationship between the three elements still fails to hold. For example, Ameskoa, a small Navarrese region bordering on Araba, was ecclesiastically divided into Lower Ameskoa, belonging to the bishopric of Iruña, and Upper Ameskoa, belonging to that of Calahorra. I don't know if different tribes inhabited each area, but toponymic and other remnants of the language yield no discernible differences, from a linguistic point of view.

In a word, it would not appear that ecclesiastical demarcations represent a continuation of the old tribal organisation, a point demonstrated by the work of Elena Barrena (1989: 283ff. and 342–343). According to Barrena, an important part of Gipuzkoa belonged to the bishopric of Baiona in ancient times and was later incorporated into Iruña, with the above-mentioned exception of the north-western zone, which included, besides Oiartzun, Irun, and Hondarribia, the towns of Pasaia, Lezo, and Errenteria.

Roldan Jimeno (2003: 64), for his part, explains the inclusion of the Gipuzkoan and Navarrese districts in the bishopric of Baiona as follows:

> Iruña's political and pastoral objectives looked to the south; the aim was to reconquer the rich Muslim territory in the Ebro Valley, and to repopulate and re-evangelise it. Economic poverty and poor communications consigned to oblivion the few inhabitants of the lands north of Belate [a mountain pass north of Navarre].[1]

Politics and economics would often seem to form the basis for ecclesiastical divisions. It is important to remember that the bishoprics were constituted after the disappearance of the Basque tribes. The bishopric of Iruña, the first one for which we have records, apparently dated back to the sixth century. It would indeed be a coincidence if the tribal boundaries recorded by Roman historians and geographers in the first and second centuries (which were in any case imprecise) should continue, several centuries later, along the same lines as in the days of the ancient tribes.

The testimony of the language

Mitxelena's point of view

In 1981, Koldo Mitxelena published an article titled "Common language and Basque dialects" in which he made a brief reference to the subject of this chapter. He defended the thesis that the dialects could not be very old and gave two reasons:

1   All the dialects share a very large number of common features, which
would be unlikely had they been truly old.
2   A large number of innovations are common to all dialects, which would
be hard to explain if the dialects had divided at an early date.

Mitxelena (1981: 311) mentioned that during the period of Roman rule
Basques in different places had probably concentrated and amalgamated, in
order to resist and counter Roman pressure:

> It is certain that linguistic Romanisation (Latinisation) in Basque-
> speaking areas would have led to [...] a drastic reduction of the area
> in which Basque was spoken, which, as a pole of attraction for
> people unable to adapt, would, especially in times of violence and
> insecurity, receive [an influx of] population from areas separated from
> the central nucleus, with the inevitable *brassage* of speakers of
> diverse dialects and varieties. This process could have lasted until the
> middle of the second century of our era, at the shortest, and much
> longer still according to the most likely estimates. What needs
> underlining is that [...] the general direction of evolution had to be
> the same: a reduction of territory and, as a result, a certain degree of
> concentration of population whose origin, and this is the important
> thing, could not help but be different.[2]

In Mitxelena's opinion, this set-of-circumstances situation would also have
shaped the development of a sense of unity among the Basques (312):

> The Roman action [...] would have contributed to an awakening of a
> certain sense of unity, and, at the very least, of safety, which would have
> grown more vigorous during the turbulent period of Visigoth rule [...], in
> which the basis for the subsequent appearance of the Navarrese mon-
> archy might possibly be found.[3]

As a consequence of these facts, Mitxelena assumed that throughout this
period the language would have tended to unify. So, the present-day dialects
were formed later, as the Basques expanded their territory and entered into
contact with speakers of other languages, and as the feeling of unity within
the framework of the Kingdom of Navarre weakened.

Whether Mitxelena's historical arguments were right or wrong, an analysis
of current Basque dialects would seem to confirm the hypothesis of their
medieval origin. Moreover, I would add a third argument in its support: the
only truly divergent dialects are the lateral ones, that is, Zuberoan, the dialect
of the Navarrese valleys of Zaraitzu and Erronkari, and the western dialect of
Araba and Bizkaia. In the central dialects, the differences are scarce and
insignificant, which would also have been unlikely if the dialects had dated
back to antiquity.

Reasons for supporting the dialects' medieval origin

The language's internal unity

Although present-day Basque is split into a large number of dialects, the number of features common to all dialects is unmistakably high. Given, as I showed in Chapter 1, that the agents acting in favour of the unity of the Basque language have, throughout its history, been barely consistent and few in number, if the division into dialects had started very early on, its commonalities would necessarily have been far fewer than is the case. In fact, the distances between the Romance languages proceeding from Latin – Castilian and Romanian, for example – are greater than those between the dialects of Basque.

Phonology

Vowels and consonants are practically the same in all the dialects, and so are the rules governing their positions and possible combinations within words. I will confine myself to presenting the main divergences. The most notable is the vowel *ü*, characteristic, above all, of the Zuberoan dialect, but whose origin seems to lie in Occitan. Zuberoan dialect has nasal vowels too, but there is evidence that the western dialect, at the other end of the country, also had such vowels in the sixteenth and seventeenth centuries, so they seem to have been rather general in relatively recent times. The same goes for the aspirated *h*, which is currently still alive in parts of the northern Basque Country, particularly in Zuberoa, but was also found in Araba in the southern part of the Basque Country, even in the fourteenth century.

The differences from dialect to dialect in Basque's abundant sibilant consonants of (*s, x, z, ts, tx, tz*) are also easily explained. In the western dialect and in many localities in the north of the province of Gipuzkoa, the pronunciation of the *s* and *z* on the one hand and of the *ts* and the *tz* on the other has become the same, but that did not happen, generally speaking, until after the sixteenth century. Zuberoan, on the other hand, has increased the number of these consonants by two. However, they arose as a result not of internal change but of borrowing from Occitan. For the different pronunciations of initial *j* in words like *yan / dxan / xan / jan* ("to eat"), it is easy to establish the following evolutionary sequence: *y> dx> x> j*. The only difference is that some dialects have evolved further along this path than others.

Apart from these differences, the rules of accentuation and intonation also vary considerably between speech communities (see Hualde 1997).

Nominal morphology

In this field, the most outstanding feature of Basque is its system of declensions, and it is precisely there that nearly all the dialectal variants can be found. The western dialect and the dialects in the northern provinces have a case absent from the other dialects – the allative of direction.* In the western dialect it is formed by the suffix -*rantza* or -*rutz* (*mendirantza* / *mendirutz* ["towards the mountain"]), and in the northern provinces by -*rat buruz* or by -*ri buruz* (*mendiari buruz*). The latter option is actually an adaptation of an Occitan usage, whereby the word *cap* ("head"), used in the same context, is replaced in Basque by the word *buru* (also "head").

The western dialect has its own suffix, -*gaz*, for the comitative case,* *lagunagaz* ("with the friend"), different from the -*kin* suffix (*lagunarekin*) used in other dialects. It would seem to be the result of an amalgamation of the general Basque components -*ga*- and -*z*, which feature, for example, in *lagunarengana* ("towards the friend, to where the friend is") and, as we have seen, *buruz* ("by means of the head, concerning the head").

Apart from that, three other suffixes vary from region to region:

a   The destinative* -*entzat* or –*endako* (*lagunarentzat* / *lagunarendako* ["for the friend"]).
b   The prolative* -*tzat* or -*tako* (*laguntzat* / *laguntako* ["as a friend"]).
c   The inessive* (in the case of animate beings) -*gan* or *baitan* ("*lagunarengan* / *lagunaren baitan*) ["in the friend"]).

Although the case system is the same in all dialects, for some cases different suffixes are employed in different dialects. A notable example concerns nominalised structures, which are in the absolutive* (-*a*) in some dialects and the genitive* (-*aren*) in others (*laguna ikustera* / *lagunaren ikustera [joan da]* ["(has left) to visit the friend"]). Nowadays, the absolutive is typical of the western and central dialects and the genitive of the eastern dialects, but it seems that in ancient times the genitive was known across the whole Basque territory. This is clear from texts from Bizkaia dating back to the seventeenth century (see Lakarra 1997: 191–192).

In more or less this same area, non-finite verbal complements of verbs such as *eman* ["give"] and *utzi* ["leave"] alternate between inessive (-*t[z]en*) and allative* (-*t[z]era*) forms. The western and central dialects have opted for the inessive (*jaten eman* ["feed"], *jaten utzi* ["allow to eat"]). The eastern dialects, on the other hand, have opted for the allative (*jatera eman, jatera utzi*).

We also find small variations in other suffixes, some of which are purely phonetic in origin. Examples include: -*ak* / -*ek* in the ergative* plural (*gizonak* / *gizonek* ["the men"]); -*ei* / -*eri* / -*er* in the dative* plural (*gizonei* / *gizoneri* / *gizoner* ["to the men"]); -*aren* / -*ain* / -*an* in the genitive* singular (*lagunaren* / *lagunain* / *lagunan* ["of the friend"]); -*kin* / -*ki* / -*kilan* in the comitative* (*gizonarekin* / *gizonareki* / *gizonarekilan* ["with the man"]); and -*tik* / -*tikan* / -*tio* / -*ti* in the ablative* (*etxetik* / *etxetikan* / *etxetio* / *etxeti* ["from home"]).

Verbal morphology

The complexity of Basque is most clearly manifested in its verbal morphology, and it is here that the dialects are at their most diverse. Even so, the differences are neither many nor particularly significant.

The main differences are to be found in the roots of some verbs. For example, the auxiliary verb of the absolutive-dative-ergative type* has three apparently different roots: *eutsi* in the western dialect, *-i* in the central zone, and *eradun* in the eastern dialects. However, in former times the region in which each of these roots was used was less strictly defined, and in many places, speakers had more than one possibility at their disposal. For example, even nowadays speakers in the Navarrese valley of Baztan use both roots, *-i* and *eradun*.

The auxiliary of the potential mode also has three different roots: *egin* across a wide area of the west of the Basque Country, *ezan*, and the eastern *iro* (*daiket* / *dezaket* / *dirot* ["I can"]). However, the root *ezan* was general until the seventeenth century. The root *egin* is also general; the sole special feature of the western region is the specialisation or grammaticalisation of *egin* as an auxiliary verb.

The distinction between the participle and the verbal radical was also general until the sixteenth or seventeenth century: the former could only be used in the indicative, for example, *hartu dugu* ("we have taken it"). Nowadays,

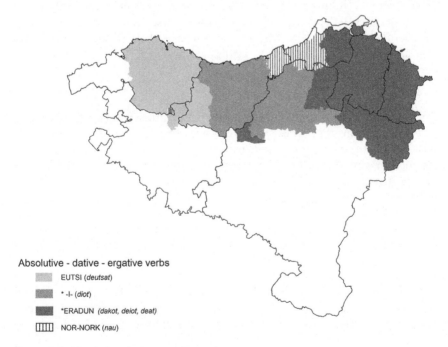

Absolutive - dative - ergative verbs

    EUTSI (*deutsat*)

    * -I- (*diot*)

    *ERADUN (*dakot, deiot, deat*)

    NOR-NORK (*nau*)

Figure 2.1 Absolutive-dative-ergative verbs

however, the participle (*hartu*) has usurped the functions of the verbal radical (*har*) across a large part of the southern Basque Country, above all in the western and central dialects.

The morpheme of the future participle divides the Basque Country in half. The western and central regions have -*go* when the radical ends in -*n*, while the eastern region has -*en: izango* / *izanen* ["will be"]. Both -*go* and -*en* are found in all dialects: -*go* is the morpheme of the locative genitive (*Berlingo* ["of Berlin"]) and -*en* is the possessive genitive (*Martinen* ["of Martin"]). So, it is a question of two different choices made within a common pool of the language.

The plural agreement morphemes vary greatly. Basque offers a wide range of possibilities, and each dialect has given priority to a single one for certain verbs. So, we have *daramaTZAt* / *daramaZKIt* ("I carry them"), *goaZ* / *goaZI* ("we go"), *diZKIo* / *dITio* / *dioZKa* / *deiTZo* / *deutsaZ* ("they have them to him/her").

There are also other differences, but they are in general trifling. Thus, for example, for the present indicative of the auxiliary verb *edun* ("have"), we have the forms *dot* (western) / *det* (Gipuzkoan) / *dut* (central-eastern) ("I have it"), which are a consequence of a different phonetic evolution, starting from a common form that can be reconstructed as **dadut*. The present forms of the auxiliary verb *izan* ("to be") are also due to a different phonetic evolution. They are *naiz* (central) / *nax* (>*nas*) (western) / *niz* (eastern) ("I am"), or *gara* (central-western) / *gera* (central) / *gira* (eastern) ("we are"). In the root of the third person singular of these verbs we also have a different vowel (-*a*- / -*e*-) in each half of the country: western and central *zan* ("was"), as against eastern *zen*.

Syntax

Strictly speaking, there are hardly any syntactic differences between dialects, and the variations that do exist have come into being since the sixteenth century. Such is the case, for example, with the use of the verb *egin* ("to do") as a support for verbal focusing, thus resembling so-called "do" support in English. It is typical, above all, of the western and central dialects, in sentences like these:

a *Mikelek erre du* "Mikel has burned it" [neutral sentence].
b *Mikelek erre egin du* "What Mikel has done is burn it" [focussing of the verbal action].

The use of the prefix *ba*- would also seem to postdate the sixteenth century. It is typical of the northern dialects and the valleys of the north of Navarre bordering on the French state. Here is an example: *Gizon batek bi seme bazituen* ("a man had two sons").

The tendency in northern dialects to invert the order "main-auxiliary verb" in constructions with focus or an interrogative pronoun also seems to postdate the sixteenth century. Instead of *nor ikusi duzu?* ("whom have you seen?") or *nik ikusi dut* ("I have seen it"), in the northern dialects it is usual to say *nor duzu ikusi?* or *nik dut ikusi.*

Lexicon

It is well known that the most striking differences between languages are in vocabulary, but even here the degree of commonality between Basque dialects is surprisingly large. The numerals, for example, are the same in all the dialects. Most of the verbs are identical. So are the adjectives. In short, many of the words that make up the patrimonial lexicon are the same. For example:

- Colours: *beltz / baltz* ("black"), *gorri* ("red"), *urdin* ("blue / gray"), *zuri* ("white"), etc.
- Parts of the body: *aho* ("mouth"), *begi* ("eye"), *belaun* ("knee"), *buru* ("head"), *oin* ("foot"), etc.
- Relations: *alaba* ("daughter"), *ahizpa* ("sister" [of girl]), *anaia* ("brother" [of boy]), *arreba* ("sister" [of boy]), *senar* ("husband"), etc.
- The nature of people: *and(e)re* ("woman"), *gizon* ("man"), *neska* ("girl"), *ume* ("child"), etc.
- Feelings: *amets* ("dream"), *esker* ("gratefulness"), *gogo* ("desire"), *lotsa* ("fear, shame"), etc.
- Places inhabited by people: *etxe* ("house"), *herri* ("village, country"), *hiri / huri* ("population nucleus"), etc.
- Household things: *ezkaratz* ("entrance hall, kitchen"), *labe* ("oven"), *leiho* ("window"), *su* ("fire"), etc.
- Tools: *aitzur* ("hoe"), *hede* ("strap"), *igitai* ("sickle"), *orratz* ("needle"), etc.
- Spatial and temporal terms and quantities: *ezker* ("left"), *ipar* ("north"), *atzo* ("yesterday"), *lehen* ("before"), *erdi* ("half"), *oso* ("whole"), etc.
- Birds, insects, and animals: *arrano* ("eagle"), *eper* ("partridge"), *erle* ("bee"), *zorri* ("louse"), *behor* ("mare"), *idi* ("ox"), *zakur / txakur* ("dog"), etc.
- Trees and plants: *belar / berar* ("grass"), *ezpel* ("boxwood"), *haltz* ("alder"), *haritz / haretx* ("oak"), etc.
- Minerals: *burdina / burnia* ("iron"), *ikatz* ("coal"), *urre* ("gold"), *zilar / zirar* ("silver"), etc.
- Food: *aza* ("cabbage"), *esne* ("milk"), *gatz* ("salt"), *gazta / gasna* ("cheese"), *haragi* ("meat"), *ogi* ("bread"), etc.
- Atmospheric phenomena: *ekaitz* ("storm"), *elur / erur* ("snow"), *euri* ("rain"), *haize* ("wind"), etc.
- Geographical features: *itsaso* ("sea"), *larre* ("meadow"), *leize* ("chasm"), *lur* ("earth"), *mendi* ("mountain"), etc.

Common innovations

In linguistics, "innovations" are changes produced within a language. In the case of Basque, many innovations that are thought to be relatively recent are common to all the dialects, thus reinforcing the hypothesis that dialectal division does not date from remote times. If the dialects were truly ancient, borrowings from Latin or from other Romance languages, as well as changes within Basque in recent times, would have evolved differently from one dialect to the other. But the opposite happened: in many cases, the result has been the same in all dialects. Examples follow.

Adaptation of loans

One of Mitxelena's most conclusive proofs that dialectal division could not have taken place in pre-Roman times is the way in which words from Latin have evolved in Basque. This evolution has generally been different from that in other surrounding languages, but it has been common to all Basque dialects. This suggests that the dialects were yet to form at the moment when these words entered the language. For example, the Latin word *pace* has produced *bake* in all the dialects of Basque (it later evolved into *pake* in the central dialect), whereas in surrounding languages French has *paix*, Occitan *patz*, Catalan *pau*, Castilian *paz*.

Here, we look at some of the rules regarding the adaptation of loans from Latin into Basque. (For more details on the rules whereby loans of Latin origin have been adapted to the Basque language, see Mitxelena 1974, 1977; Hualde 1991, 2003.)

Basque has generally avoided consonant groups of the sort known as *muta cum liquida*, that is, *p, t, k, b, d, g, f+l*, and *r*. The same procedures have been followed in all the dialects: either one of the consonants has been eliminated (Latin *pluma*> Basque *luma*), or an anaptictic vowel* has been intercalated between the consonants (Latin *cruce*> Basque *gurutze*).

In word initials, the vibrant consonant *r-* has been rejected in Basque. Usually the vowels *a-* or *e-* precede it in Basque. Common to all dialects are *errege* ("king"), *Erroma* ("Rome"), *errota* ("wheel, mill"), and *arrazoi(n)* ("reason").

Other Basque adaptations, again common to all dialects, are the change from *p-, t-*, and *k-* initials to *b-, d-*, and *g-*: *tempora*> *denbora* ("time"), *causa*> *gauza* ("thing"), and *cella*> *gela* ("room, cell"). In the intervocalic position we have the loss of *-n-* (*corona*> *koroa* ["crown"]), the passage from *l* to *r* (*angelu*> *aingeru* ["angel"]), and the passage from *-nn-* to *-n-* and *-ll-* to *-l-* (*annona*> *anoa* ["portion"] and *castellu*> *gaztelu* ["castle"]).

Most of the Latin loans are identical in all Basque dialects. Here are some examples: *eremu* ("desert, wilderness"), *eskola* ("school"), *ezpata* ("sword"), *gorputz* ("body"), *joko* ("game"), *katea* ("chain"), *landare* ("plant"), *madarikatu* ("cursed"), *olio* ("oil"), *piper* ("pepper"), *soka* ("rope"), *zuku* ("juice"), and so on. Many of these words entered into Basque very recently, by way of Romance languages. Such is the case, for example, with *altxatu* ("to raise"), *arraza* ("race"), *arropa* ("clothes"), *balio* ("value"), *bota* ("throw"), *leku* ("place"), *mendebal* ("[wind from the] west"), *polit* ("pretty"), *sob(e)ra* ("excessive"), *soinu* ("sound"), *teila* ("tile").

Compound words

Compound and derived words cannot be very old. As Mitxelena pointed out, the changes that have taken place in the first element in such formations are the same in all the dialects. Some examples follow.

- When the first element ends in *di* / -gi, it becomes -t: *ardi* ("sheep") > *artzain* ("shepherd"), *begi* ("eye") > *betile* ("eyelash").
- When the first element ends in -gu, it becomes -t: *sagu* ("mouse") > *sator* ("mole").
- When the final vowel is -e, -o, or -u, it becomes -a: *ate* ("door") > *atari* ("entrance hall"), *baso* ("forest") > *basajaun* ("lord of the forest" [a mythological figure]), and *katu* ("cat") > *katakume* ("kitten").
- Endings in -n become -r: *egun* ("day") > *eguraldi* ("time"), *jaun* ("lord") > *jauregi* ("palace"), and *oihan* ("forest") > *oiharbide* ("forest road").
- Endings in -ra, -re, and -ri become -l: *euskara* ("Basque language") > *euskaldun* ("Basque speaker"), *abere* ("beast") > *abeletxe* ("cowshed"), and *afari* ("dinner") > *afaldu* ("to have dinner").
- Endings in -ri and -ru lose the vowel: *herri* ("country") > *erbeste* ("foreign country"), *iturri* ("source") > *iturburu* ("spring"), and *buru* ("head") > *burmuin* ("brain").
- Words of more than two syllables ending in -o lose that vowel: *itsaso* ("sea") > *itsasbazter* ("seashore, coast").

Other changes

Other changes seem to be more recent and affect all the dialects. The most notable is the creation of a complex verbal system used between people who know each other and between whom there is a relationship of trust. These verbal inflections also vary according to the gender of the person to whom they are directed. For example, the verbal inflection of the courteous or neutral *naiz* ("I am") becomes *nauk* (masculine) or *naun* (feminine) in the case of relationships of friendship and trust. Similarly, *dakit* ("I know") becomes *zakiat* / *zakinat*, and so on. Except for a few small differences, these inflections have an identical structure in all the dialects. In linguistic work, this phenomenon is known as allocutive conjugation.

The ancient second person plural (e.g., *zu zara* ["you (plural) are"]) has become singular ("you [singular] are") (cf. the evolution in English of the relationship between "thou" and "you") and is traditionally used among people who wish to maintain a degree of detachment and respect. The plural verb has, as a result, acquired a new form (*zuek zarete* ["you (plural) are"]). This process affects all verbs and all dialects.

The similarity of the central dialects

I have already pointed out that the truly divergent dialects are the lateral ones, and that there is a large degree of unity among the central dialects. However, not every kind of divergence necessarily demonstrates the antiquity of the dialects. Innovations are the most important potential indicator. The greater the quantity and quality of the innovations, the greater the likelihood that the dialects are ancient. On the other hand, if they were few in number and of scant importance, one could more or less rest assured that the dialects are recent. In a word, the number and importance of the innovations will give us an idea of the moment of formation of the dialects.

Applying this criterion to the lateral dialects, we see that the speech forms of the valleys of Zaraitzu and Erronkari have hardly had any innovations of their own. On the whole, they have borrowed from Zuberoan and other Navarrese dialects in the surrounding regions. Beyond that, they borrowed copiously from Navarrese-Aragonese Romance, as well as adopting notable archaisms, as in the case of the demonstratives, which have an initial *k-*, as in *kaur* ("this"), *kori* ("that [near]"), and *kura* ("that" [distant]) (compared with the standard forms *hau, hori,* and *hura*).

As for the innovations produced within dialects, I will mention only four, although they are also of scant significance:

1   In two towns in the southern part of the Erronkari Valley, Bidankoze and Garde, when words ending in *-u* gained the article *-a*, the result was *-iua* in Bidankoze and *-ioa* in Garde, e.g., *buriua* / *burioa* ("the head") instead of the standard *burua*. This is not an unusual and isolated development. In large swathes of the eastern part of the Basque Country *u* + *a* has resulted in *-uya*, e.g., *buruya*. What subsequently happened in the two places in the Erronkari Valley was a simple metathesis, whereby *-uya>* *-iua* / *-ioa*.

2   In the Erronkari Valley, *i* commonly became *x* in intervocalic position: *anaia> anaxea* ("brother"), *leiho> lexo* ("window"), etc.

3   Also, in the Erronkari Valley, the morpheme of the verbal noun was usually *-(e)tan: biltan* ("picking up") and *xatan* ("eating"). The suffix *-eta* is a common feature of the language, and in some parts of Bizkaia, at the other end of the country, it is used with the same meaning: *apurtan* ("breaking"), *garbitan* ("cleaning"), etc.

4   In the Zaraitzu Valley, when words ending in *-a* gained the article *-a*, the result was *-a* + *a>* *-ara*, e.g., *uskara* ("Basque language") + *a>* *uskarara*

("the Basque language"). But this too is neither surprising nor original, for in neighbouring Zuberoa and the Erronkari Valley the result has been *-a* + *-a*> *-áa*, which was then reduced to a simple *-á*. Consequently, in the Zaraitzu Valley the actual innovation was simply to intercalate the consonant *-r-* between the two vowels.

So apart from the dialect of these two Navarrese valleys, only Zuberoan and the western dialects truly diverge. However, as I go on to show in the next chapter, neither dialect – especially not Zuberoan – is particularly rich in innovations. Many of the divergences are due to the preservation of archaisms or to loans from neighbouring languages.

In the case of Zuberoan, it must be borne in mind that Occitan, in its Bearnese Gascon variety, was the official language of Zuberoa between the fourteenth and the sixteenth centuries, and that practically up until the first half of the twentieth century it was known and even used by a large number of people in Zuberoa. That is why so many Occitan features entered into Zuberoan. An example is the vowel *ü*, so characteristic of that dialect.

Dialectal division in medieval times

Basque was already divided into dialects in the sixteenth century, as evidenced in the first relatively extensive written texts from a relatively wide spread of places that we have from that period. It is therefore likely that dialectal fragmentation went on throughout the Middle Ages.

I will deal with some of the differences in the next chapter, but it is a striking fact that already in the sixteenth century certain features appeared that split the Basque Country into three. On the one hand, Araba, Bizkaia, and Gipuzkoa were separated from Navarre and the northern provinces. On the other hand, the three northern provinces were separated from the four southern ones.

Why did this happen? Did it have anything to do with the fragmentation of the Kingdom of Navarre in the eleventh and twelfth centuries? We cannot say for sure, but the fact is that from then on, the provinces of Lapurdi and Zuberoa were oriented socially and economically towards places north of the Pyrenees. Araba, Bizkaia, and Gipuzkoa, meanwhile, were integrated into the Kingdom of Castile, and their relations with Navarre were, thereafter, neither cordial nor even moderately friendly. The reordering of the Basque provinces in those years could have shaped the later evolution of the language and might have played an important and decisive role in the dialectalisation of Basque.

Eastern and central-western features

Among the features that separated the central-western dialects of the provinces of Araba, Bizkaia, and Gipuzkoa, already integrated into the Kingdom of Castile, from the eastern dialects of Navarre and the northern provinces, are the following seven:

Erronkari and Zaraitzu Valleys

Figure 2.2 Erronkari and Zaraitzu valleys

1   In the central-western dialects the consonant group -*st*- is used in words like *beste* ("other"), *bost* ("five"), *este* ("intestine"), and *ost*- ("sky, firmament"), a component of words like *ostegun* ("Thursday") and *ostiral* ("Friday"), for example. In the eastern dialects, on the other hand, except for Zuberoan and nearby dialects, we find the group -*rtz*- in this set of words: *bertze, bortz, ortzegun, ortziral,* and *(h)ertze,* the latter being a general variant throughout the eastern area.

2   In the central-western dialects the inessive* suffix for animate beings is -*gan,* as against *baitan* in the eastern dialects: *lagunarengan / lagunaren baitan* ("in the friend").

3   Except for some isolated cases, the noun complement is constructed with the absolutive* (-*a*) in the central-western dialects and the possessive genitive* (-*aren*) in the eastern ones: *laguna ikustera* ("to visit the friend") as against *lagunaren ikustera* (literally, "to the visiting of the friend").

4   In the eastern dialects, the unconjugated verbal complements of certain verbs (*ausartu / menturatu* ["dare"], *eman* ["give"], *saiatu* ["try"], *utzi* ["permit"], etc.) are used in the allative case* -*t(z)era,* as against the central-western dialects, which opted for the inessive -*t(z)en.* In the poetry of the Lower Navarrese priest Bernat Etxepare, author of the first book printed in Basque, in 1545, we find the following examples (Etxepare 1545):

assayatu bere lengoage propriaren favoretan heuscaraz cerbait obra egui-tera ("to endeavor to write some works in Basque, in defense of one's language")

(prologue: 9–10)

finian ere eztic uzten harc galcera beria ("never permit the loss of one's own")
(ii: 72)

neure penen erraytera are eniz ausarcen ("I do not even dare to count my sorrows").

(v: 12)

5   In the root of the third-person singular of the verb *izan* ("to be") we find *-a* in the central-western dialects and *-e-* in the eastern ones. The central-western verbal inflections are *dan / dala* ("which is") and *dalako* ("because it is") in the present and *zan / zala* ("which was") and *zalako* ("because it was") in the past. In the eastern dialects, there is *den, dela, delako(tz), zen, zela*, and *zelako(tz)*.

6   The morpheme of the future participle is *-go* in the central-western dialects and *-en* in the eastern ones: *izango / izanen* ("will be").

7   In the eastern dialects the variant *-elarik* is used in temporal and modal sentences, in addition to the general *-ela*, the only option in the central-western dialects. In a letter addressed by the Protestant minister Joanes Leizarraga to the Queen of Béarn and Lower Navarre, Joana of Albret, in 1571, we find among others the following examples (Leizarraga 1571):

ni çure eçagun gabea beçala naicelaric ("being unknown to you")
orain çure moienez reedificatzen delaric ("now that thanks to your intervention it is being rebuilt").

Northern and southern features

The six main differences, observable as early as the sixteenth century, between the northern and southern dialects of Vasconia are as follows.

1   The aspirated sound had been completely lost from the southern dialects even before the sixteenth century, with the probable exception of some northern Navarrese dialects close to the northern provinces. Aspiration is still a feature of the speech of Navarre's Luzaide Valley.

2   The passage from *o-* to *u-* before nasal consonants was already a feature of the northern dialects. Bernat Etxepare (1545) offers the following examples: *huin* (cf. *oin*) ("foot"), *hun* ("good"), *unsa* (cf. *ontsa*) ("well"), and *undar* (cf. *hondar*) ("last"). In the demonstratives, there was *hunek*

("this"), *hunen* ("of this"), *huneki* ("with this"), and *hunat* ("here") (cf. *honek, honen, honekin, hona*).

3   Different ways of incorporating words from Romance languages into Basque were used on either side of the border. In the northern provinces, the loss of the final -*e* by apocope in loans was offset by the introduction of the vowel -*a*. Etxepare (1545), for example, writes *adbokata* ("lawyer"), *demandanta* ("plaintiff"), *deshonesta* ("dishonest"), *elementa* ("element"), and *pazienza* ("patience"), which in the southern dialects are *abogadu, demandante, desonesto, elementu,* and *pazienzia*.

4   In the allative case* suffix, the variant -*rat* already appears in the northern dialects (-*ra* in the southern ones), although less frequently than at present. In the poetry of Etxepare (1545), one finds *norat* ("whither"), *aitzinerat* ("forward"), and the demonstratives *hunat* ("here"), *horrat* ("there" [near]), and *harat* ("there" [distant]).

5   Within the series of intensive personal pronouns, we find the *zuhaur* type ("you yourself") in the northern texts. In Etxepare's poetry, we have *nihaur* ("I myself"), *ihaurk / ihaurorrek* ("you yourself" [familiar]), *guhaur* ("we ourselves"), and *zuhaurk / zuhaurorrek* ("you yourself" [polite]). The exception was probably the Lapurdian coast, where (at least in seventeenth-century texts) we find forms of the *zerori* ("you yourself") type, as in most of Gipuzkoa and Navarre.

6   Already in the sixteenth century we find relative sentences formed with "naked" participles, i.e., without any inflection, of a sort typical of the northern dialects. In the southern dialects, the corresponding verbal inflection was used, or the participle was accompanied by -*tako*, -*riko*, or -*rikako*. The poet Etxepare (1545) provides the following example (I: 436): *Eguin oroz recibitu neure merexituya* ("to receive what is due to me for all [the acts] that I have committed").

Accordingly, what in Etxepare's language was *egin* (*oroz*) ("for all that I have committed") was in the southern dialects *egin ditudan / egindako / eginiko / eginikako*.

Dialectal division starting in the eighteenth century

As I will go on to explain in Chapter 5, during the eighteenth and nineteenth centuries several literary dialects formed within the Basque language: Gipuzkoan, Zuberoan, two types of Bizkaian, and, in the twentieth century, Navarrese-Lapurdian. As a result of the emergence of these literary models, which were more or less provincial in scope, writers in each region lost sight of the language as a whole and started giving priority to endless localisms and recent innovations that had been fermenting in each of the dialects.

The intervention of Prince Bonaparte and his collaborators in the nineteenth century proved to be decisive. The Prince's eagerness to demarcate clearly and precisely the dialects and subdialects and even speech communities that he considered special led to the further strengthening of these frontiers.

In short, these developments, taken as a whole, led the dialects to follow a divergent course starting in the eighteenth century, so that the distances between them widened.

Conclusions

In this chapter, I have argued that the present Basque dialects seem to have originated in the Middle Ages. The critical moment in the dialectal division lay perhaps between the eleventh and twelfth centuries, when the Kingdom of Navarre fractured and started to decline. It is likely, however, that the western area (Araba, Bizkaia, and Gipuzkoa's Deba Valley) and the eastern area (Zuberoa and the Navarrese valleys of Zaraitzu and Erronkari) had already distanced themselves from the rest of the Basque regions at a still earlier date.

The argument that the present Basque dialects have their origin in a remote age, before the arrival of the Romans, and coincide with regions occupied by ancient Basque tribes does not seem sustainable. First, the essential unity of the language, especially its central dialects, is beyond doubt. Second, a large number of innovations, common to all dialects, arose after the arrival of the Romans. Third, the truly divergent dialects are the two lateral ones, Zuberoan and the western dialect group. Fourth, the innovations are not particularly striking. Generally speaking, the differences between dialects consist of different choices from a common stock of language. Fifth and finally, with the exception of the western region, the borders of the remaining dialects do not coincide with the confines usually assigned to the ancient tribes, nor with those that enclosed the early ecclesiastical dioceses.

Notes

1 Los objetivos políticos y pastorales de Pamplona miraban hacia el sur; el rico territorio musulmán del valle del Ebro era el objetivo a reconquistar, repoblar y reevangelizar. La pobreza económica y las malas comunicaciones relegaban al olvido a los escasos habitantes que malvivían en las tierras situadas al norte de Belate.
2 Es seguro que la romanización lingüística (la latinización) en zonas éuskaras de lengua tuvo que suponer (...) una reducción drástica del área de habla vasca que, como foco de atracción de gentes inadaptadas, tuvo que recibir sobre todo en épocas de violencia y de inseguridad población de zonas separadas del núcleo central, con el inevitable *brassage* de hablantes de dialectos y variedades muy diversas. Aquí se alude a un proceso que pudo durar hasta mediados del siglo II de nuestra era, en la cronología más corta, y bastante más, según las estimaciones más probables. Lo que se quiere subrayar es que (...) el sentido general de la evolución tuvo que ser el mismo: reducción del territorio y, por ello

mismo, alguna concentración de población cuya procedencia, y esto es lo importante, no podía menos de ser diversa.

3 La acción romana (...) pudo contribuir a despertar un cierto sentido de unidad, y en todo caso, de seguridad, que se vigorizará durante la etapa turbulenta de la dominación visigoda (...), puesto que en él se halla posiblemente la base de la posterior aparición de la monarquía navarra.

References

Allières, Jacques. 1981. "La dialectologie basque". *Euskal linguistika eta literatura: bide berriak*:103–113. Bilbao: Universidad de Deusto.

Alvarez Enparantza, José Luis (Txillardegi) and Gotzon Aurrekoetxea (dir.) 1987. *Euskal dialektologiaren hastapenak*. Bilbao: Udako Euskal Unibertsitatea.

Arejita, Adolfo, Ander Manterola and Segundo Oar-Arteta. 2007. *Euskararen geografia historikoa*. Gasteiz: Gobierno Vasco.

Barrena, Elena. 1989. *La formación histórica de Guipúzcoa*. Donostia: Cuadernos Universitarios, Sección Historia, n° 5, E.U.T.G.- Mundaiz.

Caro Baroja, Julio. 1943. *Los pueblos del norte de la Península Ibérica*. Madrid: Consejo Superior de Investigaciones Científicas.

Caro Baroja, Julio. 1945. *Materiales para una historia de la lengua vasca en su relación con la latina*. Salamanca: Universidad de Salamanca.

Etxepare, Bernat. 1545. *Linguae Vasconum Primitiae*. (P. Altuna, ed.) Bilbao: Mensajero, 1980.

Hualde, José Ignacio. 1991. *Basque Phonology*. London: Routledge.

Hualde, José Ignacio. 1997. *Euskararen azentuerak. Anejos del Anuario del Seminario de Filología Vasca "Julio de Urquijo"*, n° 42. Donostia and Bilbao: Diputación Foral de Gipuzkoa and Universidad del País Vasco.

Hualde, José Ignacio. 2003. "Phonology". (J. I. Hualde and J. Ortiz de Urbina, eds.) *A Grammar of Basque*:15–112. Berlin and New York: Mouton de Gruyter.

Jimeno, Roldán. 2003. *Los orígenes del cristianismo en la tierra de los vascones*. Iruña: Pamiela.

Lakarra, Joseba Andoni. 1997. *Refranes y sentencias (1596). Ikerketak eta edizioa*. Bilbao: Real Academia de la Lengua Vasca.

Larramendi, Manuel. 1745. *Diccionario trilingüe del castellano, bascuence y latín*. Donostia: Bartolomé Riesgo y Montero.

Leizarraga, Joanes. 1571. *Jesus Christ gure Jaunaren Testamendu Berria*. La Rochelle: Pierre Hautin. Facsímil: Donostia, Hordago, 1979.

Mitxelena, Koldo. 1974. "El elemento latino-románico en la lengua vasca". *Fontes Linguae Vasconum*, 6, n° 17, 183–209. Iruña: Institución Príncipe de Viana.

Mitxelena, Koldo. 1977. *Fonética histórica vasca*. Second revised edition. Donostia: Diputación Foral de Gipuzkoa.

Mitxelena, Koldo. 1981. "Lengua común y dialectos vascos". *Anuario del Seminario de Filología Vasca "Julio de Urquijo"*, 15: 289–313. Donostia: Diputación Foral de Gipuzkoa.

Mujika, Serapio. 1914–1917. "El obispado de Bayona con relación a los pueblos de Guipúzcoa adscritos a dicha diócesis". Reprinted in *Revista Internacional de Estudios Vascos*, 8: 185–229. Bilbao: La Gran Enciclopedia Vasca, 1969.

Oihenart, Arnaut. 1656. *Notitia utriusque Vasconiae tum Ibericae tum Aquitanicae.* Second revised edition. Translated by Javier Gorosterratzu. *Revista Internacional de Estudios Vascos,* 17–19. Bilbao: La Gran Enciclopedia Vasca, 1971–1972.

Pagola, Rosa Miren. 1991. *Dialektologiaren atarian (Euskal dialektologiara hurbilketa).* Bilbao: Mensajero.

Pagola, Rosa Miren. 1992. "Euskara eta euskalkiak lehen eta orain". *Euskalki literarioak*: 37–59. Bilbao: Labayru Ikastegia.

3   Centres of innovation

I said in the previous chapter that the present Basque dialects seem to have originated in medieval times, but it remains to be explained where the innovations first emerged. This is barely explored terrain. The first person to broach this subject was the historian Elena Barrena (1989: 110ff.). She proposed three places in which the dialects might have formed, in three mountain massifs: Gorbeia, between Araba and Bizkaia; Aralar, between Gipuzkoa and Navarre; and Saioa, between Navarre, Lapurdi, and Lower Navarre.

However, given the area covered by the dialects (see Zuazo 2013, 2014), it would seem that their formation cannot be explained in the way Barrena suggests. The present-day dialects of Basque are more likely to have emerged in urban centres than in the mountains. As I see it, the main innovative foci would have been Iruña-Pamplona, Vitoria-Gasteiz, central Bizkaia, Zuberoa, and Lower Navarre (in the east), and the Beterri region in Gipuzkoa.

Iruña-Pamplona

Iruña was undoubtedly the most important Basque city in ancient times. By the sixth century, a bishopric had already been established there (Larrea 1996), and Iruña was an important communications hub at an early date – the Roman road that linked Bordeaux with Astorga passed through Iruña. Later, the Santiago road also passed through the city. Iruña maintained its hegemony within the Basque Country until the sixteenth century (Monteano 2017).

The linguistic innovations listed in the previous chapter, which affected all the Basque dialects, may have had their origin in Iruña, although it cannot be ruled out that other important nuclei of population outside the Basque Country as now constituted, including the Aquitaine region, also played a role. What one can say with some assurance is that these processes began at a very early stage. Other innovations, undoubtedly more modern, pertain to a smaller area, and their focus seems to have also been Iruña. Among the latter innovations were at least three, which I now discuss.

1   When an article was joined to words ending in *-a*, the result was *-a + a> -a*.
     So, for example, *luma* ("feather") + *a* produces *luma*. This innovation
     spread to most of the province of Navarre, except for the valleys of
     Zaraitzu and Erronkari, at the eastern end, and the region of Burunda to
     the west. It also covers the whole of the provinces of Lapurdi and Lower
     Navarre and the eastern half of Gipuzkoa. As I mentioned in the previous
     chapter, at the eastern end the result was *-áa> -á* in Zuberoa (*lümá*) and in
     Erronkari (*lumá*) and *-ara* in Zaraitzu (*lumara*). In the next section we will
     see that in the western area the result was *-ea* (*lumea*).

2   The morpheme of the second-person plural of verbs of the absolutive
     type* is *-te: zarete* ("you [plural] are"), *zineten* ("you [plural] were"),
     zaitezte ("you [plural] be [imperative]"), *zabiltzate* ("you [plural] go"),
     zaudete ("you [plural] are"), etc. Its distribution largely resembles that of
     the previous phenomenon, with the following differences: in Gipuzkoa its
     extent is greater, for only the Deba Valley is largely unaffected; in
     Navarre, on the other hand, not only Burunda but almost the whole of
     the Sakana region are unaffected. In these lateral dialects, the plural
     morpheme is usually *-(i)e: zarie / zidie* ("you are").

3   It seems likely that the morpheme of the imperfective aspect *-tzen* was
     consolidated and developed in Iruña. Evidence can be found in the book
     Tratado de como se ha de oyr missa ("Treatise on how we ought to hear
     the mass") by Juan de Beriain (1621), a native of Uterga, in the Iruña
     basin, published in 1621. In the lateral zones – to simplify, in Zuberoa,
     Araba, and Bizkaia – the variant *-ten* has a wider distribution. For
     example, *jarten* ("sitting") is used instead of *jartzen* and *ibilten / ebilten*
     ("walking") instead of *ibiltzen*. In the northern provinces, the ending *-iten*
     is still usually used instead of *-ten: emaiten* ("giving") (for *ematen*).

Vitoria-Gasteiz

The current state of knowledge of the Basque language in Araba

Until recently, Araba's role in the history and evolution of Basque was not
sufficiently valued. There was little evidence of the language in that province,
and the evidence that did exist was of unknown provenance.

Historical references to the Basque language of Araba are also sparse
and vague. Arnaut Oihenart (1656 [1971]: 353), in the seventeenth century,
classified the speech of Gipuzkoa and Araba as belonging to one and the
same dialect. In the eighteenth century, Manuel Larramendi (1729: 12)
emphasised the "mixed" character of Araba Basque in his grammar, but in
his dictionary (Larramendi 1745: xxvii) he affirmed that "in general its
dialect is Bizkaian." In the *Corografía de Gipuzkoa*, written in the middle
of the same century (Larramendi 1969: 299 [Tellechea Idigoras, ed.]), he
insisted on the unity of Araban and Bizkaian, but added that there were
some differences.

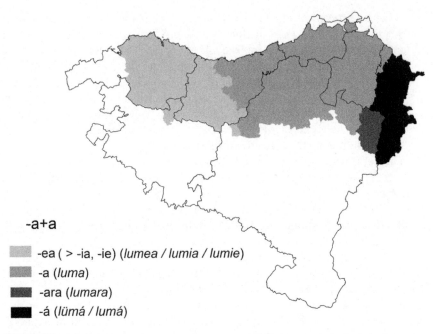

-a+a

◻ -ea (> -ia, -ie) (*lumea / lumia / lumie*)
◻ -a (*luma*)
◼ -ara (*lumara*)
◼ -á (*lümá / lumá*)

Figure 3.1 -a + a

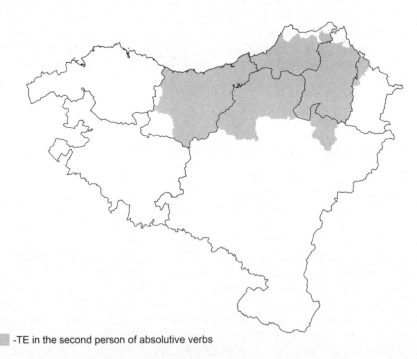

◻ -TE in the second person of absolutive verbs

Figure 3.2 -te in the second person of absolutive verbs.

At the start of the nineteenth century, the Franciscan friar Pedro Antonio Añibarro (1969: 12 [Villasante, ed.]) again mentioned the mixed character of Araban Basque and, as early as the middle of the century, Prince Bonaparte (1867: 7) classified it as part of the Bizkaian dialect.

None of the people mentioned here made the slightest mention of the features of Araban Basque, while all provided abundant information regarding the language spoken elsewhere. Nor did I come across any references in the writings of the Jesuit Agustín Kardaberatz, who toured Araba as a missionary and was sensitive to language issues.

However, things changed in the second half of the twentieth century. Gerardo López de Guereñu began, in 1956, publishing lists of place names and other words collected across the length and breadth of Araba (López de Guereñu 1989, 1998). In 1958, Koldo Mitxelena and Manuel Agud published a dictionary that the Italian Niccolò Landucci commissioned in 1562, and that had remained unpublished (Landucci 1562). In the foreword, Mitxelena pointed out that two of Landucci's Basque collaborators might have been Araban, perhaps even from Gasteiz.

Placing Landucci's dictionary in Araba opened the doors to further research, and new evidence of Araban Basque began to appear: the poet Juan Bautista Gamiz (1696–1773) from Sabando (Goikoetxea 1984); Julián García de Albeniz from Araia, author of a short translation from Castilian into Basque in 1778 (Altuna Otegi 1995); and Juan Pérez de Lazarraga from Larrea, author of an extensive literary work, written around 1564, which came to light in 2004 (Pérez de Lazarraga 2004). It has also become evident that certain authors who had been thought to be from other places were in fact, or might have been, Araban. Among them was Juan Pérez de Betolatza, born in Betolatza, who translated a catechism into Basque in 1596 (Pérez de Betolatza 1596).

Other Araban wrote short compositions or loose words and sentences in Basque. They included Gaspar Gamarra (1648), Juan Luzuriaga (1686) and Simón Martínez Ochoa (1695) (Knörr 1998 and Altuna Otegi 2002). To all this testimony we must add materials collected in the few places in Araba where Basque has remained alive: in Zigoitia, in the first half of the twentieth century (Barandiaran 1973: 71–72 and 273–274, Knörr 2005); and, more recently, in Aramaio (Pujana 1979 and Ormaetxea 2006) and Legutio (Carrera and García 2005). We also have new toponymic material collected by José Antonio González Salazar (1985–1998).

Thanks to the data now available, we can get an idea of what Basque was like in Araba – a very basic and superficial one, but one that at least covers an important part of its territory. Particularly interesting are the testimonies from the eastern end of the province (Juan Bautista Gamiz and Julián García de Albeniz), which help us to show the extent to which certain Western innovations had penetrated this region.

Studies of the speech communities of Gipuzkoa and Navarre, bordering on Araba, have yielded a number of surprises. These include the material collected in the Deba Valley and the Goierri region, in Gipuzkoa, and in the regions of Burunda, Ameskoa, and Lana, in Navarre. Progress has also been made in our knowledge of the state of Basque in various periods in parts of Burgos and La Rioja, starting with the work of José J. Bautista Merino Urrutia (1978). The presence in these areas of features previously considered Bizkaian has forced a rethink regarding their origin.

Innovative focus

The fact that certain linguistic phenomena are observed in Araba, Bizkaia, the western half of Gipuzkoa (the Deba Valley, Goierri, and Urola), the western regions of Navarre (Burunda, Ameskoa, and Lana), La Rioja, and Burgos renders a Bizkaian origin for them unlikely. There are no historical facts to explain this diffusion. However, the difficulties melt away if we start out from Gasteiz. At least since the mid-eleventh century, Gasteiz has been the key enclave in the western region, capable of spreading the innovations across a wide domain. It seems that at the end of the eleventh century, Gasteiz had a walled enclosure that gave it a certain prominence, amid a broad stretch of territory dotted with villages. But we must also take into account the role played by the bishopric of Araba in the eleventh century (see Azka-rate and Solaun 2009 and García-Gómez 2017).

Extant sources of the Araba variety of Basque

Figure 3.3 Extant sources of the Araba variety of Basque

Bizkaia, on the other hand, could boast of no such nuclei until much later. Iñaki García Camino (2002) shows that the areas with the highest population density in early medieval times were in the foothills of the Oiz and Sollube mountains, particularly in what is today the Durangaldea and the Urdaibai region.

Finally, I should add in passing that a similar kind of Basque was apparently spoken in the western districts of Navarre (Burunda, Ameskoa, and Lana) and the eastern part of Araba. If so, the thesis regarding the relationship between dialect, tribe, and ecclesiastical diocesis would once again be called into question. The explanation for this coincidence of language would probably be that they were influenced by both Iruña and Gasteiz and, logically, by the close economic, commercial, and social ties maintained by their inhabitants, despite belonging to two different ecclesiastical dioceses (Calahorra and Iruña) and even to two different kingdoms (Castile and Navarre). In my opinion, it is these relationships that explain dialectal boundaries, rather than old tribal and ecclesiastical divisions. Further north, in the Gipuzkoan counties of Goierri and Urola, the same dual influence of Gasteiz and Iruña can be observed.

Regarding the innovations that in all probability started in Gasteiz, they all exceed the usual limits of the western dialect (Araba, Bizkaia, and the Deba Valley) and extend, even though their regions or isoglosses do not always coincide, to the Gipuzkoan areas of Goierri and Urola and the Navarrese areas of Burunda, Lana, and Ameskoa. There follow five such innovations.

1   When words ending in -*a* are joined to the singular article, the result has been -*a* + *a*> -*ea*, which subsequently evolved into -*ia* or -*ie*. For example, the translation by Julián García de Albeniz (1778) has *arimea* ("soul") (cf. standard *arima*).

2   Use of the morpheme -*rik* in expressions of the type *etxerik etxe* ("from house to house"), *kalerik kale* ("from street to street, through the streets"). The standard, and Western, form is -*z: etxez etxe, kalez kale*. Landucci's dictionary (Landucci 1562) translated the Spanish expression *grada a grada* ("step by step") as *gradayc grada*.

3   Replacement of the **ezan* root by *egin*. At present, *egin* rules supreme in the western dialect, and only partially in most of Gipuzkoa and in the Sakana region in Navarre. Juan Pérez de Betolatza's catechism (Pérez de Betolatza 1596) has *libradu gaguizuz* ("free us") (cf. standard *libra gaitzazu*).

4   Substitution of the verb radical by the participle. Today, that process has spread across the whole of Gipuzkoa and the western part of Navarre. In those areas, however, speakers still sporadically use the verbal radical, but without any clear awareness of their actual spheres and functions. Landucci's dictionary, for example, translates Spanish *cosa sanable* ("a thing that can be cured") as *osatu diten gauçea*, whereby the participle *osatu* replaces the verb radical *osa*.

Present-day area where *a + a* > *-ea / -ia / -ie*

Figure 3.4 Present-day area where -a + a> -ea (> -ia, -ie)

5   Treatment of the verbs *irten* ("to leave") and *igo(n)* ("to go up") as verbs of the absolutive-ergative type,* instead of the absolutive general.* Both verbs feature in this fragment by Juan Pérez de Lazarraga ([2004]c.1564):

> *acabaduric, bada, Silveroc bere cantaetea, urten eben bere camararean eta ygo eben bere ugaçabaren aposentura* ("Silvero, having finished his singing session, left his room and went up to his master's room").

So *urten eben* ("went out") and *ygo eben* ("went up") replace the standard *irten zen* and *igo zen*.

Other Araban innovations

The phenomena presented below are less widely distributed. Usually, they are confined to Bizkaia and the Deba Valley (but not all its northern part), while in some respects the eastern part of Araba itself is not affected. Even so, its origin is best explained by starting from Araba rather than from Bizkaia.

Although many innovations began in Araba, they reached their fullest development in Bizkaia. In Araba, two forms coexist, one general to all the dialects and the other typically western, but in Bizkaia only the second sort occurs. The following list of important innovations, 13 in all, show that the western region has served as a very active nucleus.

1 The vowel *i*, as the second member of a diphthong, has palatalised the consonants *z* and *tz* that follow it, converting them into *x* and *tx* respectively, and the *i* itself has subsequently disappeared. The toponymy of much of the province of Araba, though not in the eastern part, is rich in examples: *aretx* ("oak") (cf. standard *har(e)itz*), *atx* ("rock") (cf. *haitz*), *elexa* ("church") (cf. *el(e)iza*), *lexar* ("ash-tree") (cf. *l(e)izar*). *Bakotx* ("only") (cf. *bakoitz*) and *kerexea* ("cherry tree") (cf. *gerezia*) are common throughout Araba. Most of these variants are also documented in Landucci's dictionary (1562) (*arecha, acha, elexa, vaquocha, querexea*), together with *achurra* ("hoe") (cf. *aitzurra*), *axea* ("wind") (cf. *haizea*), *axcorea* ("ax") (cf. *aizkora*), *gach* ("illness") (cf. *gaitz*), *guoxa* ("tomorrow / early") (cf. *goiza*), *nox* ("when") (cf. *noiz*), and *nax* ("I am") (cf. *naiz*).

2 The suffix *-gaz* of the comitative case* probably originated in Araba. It is present, for example, in the verses of Juan Bautista Gamiz and in the translation by Julián García de Albeniz, both from the eastern end of the province: *alcarregaz* ("together") and *bategaz* ("with one"), written by Gamiz in the eighteenth century. However, this suffix did not displace the common *-kin*, which is habitually found in Landucci's dictionary (Landucci 1562). In Bizkaia, on the other hand, *-gaz* is the sole option, although in the eastern part of Bizkaia *-kin* is used in the plural. The catechism of the Araban Juan Pérez de Betolatza (1596) also has *-gaz* (singular) and *-kaz* (plural) as the sole option.

3 The western dialect has a special suffix to indicate the allative of direction.* Landucci frequently documents words with the suffix *-rutz:* *asçerusç* ("backwards"), *barrurusç* ("inwards"), *escubirusç* ("towards the right"), *ezquerrerusç* ("towards the left"), *gorusç* ("upwards"), *verusç* ("downwards"), *norusç* ("whither"), etc. The suffix survives in the Deba Valley and in the eastern part of Bizkaia, and also occurs throughout Gipuzkoa and the western regions of Navarre, but only in the deictic adverbs*: *honutz* ("hither"), *horrutz* ("thither [near]"), and *harutz* ("thither [distant]"). In the Bizkaia interior, the variant *-rantza* is used.

4 In western Basque, in ancient times a special suffix was used in the ablative case*: *-rean*. It seems to be an amalgam of two morphemes common to all dialects: the genitive *-re* and the inessive *-an*. Landucci has numerous instances: *arean* ("from there"), *urrutirean* ("from afar"), *dolençiarean convaleçidu* ("convalescence from pain"), etc.

5 Verbal nouns that are final-type complements with verbs of movement are constructed in the inessive case. Juan Pérez de Betolatza's catechism has the following example:

> *Aric etorrico da juzgaetan hilac eta viciac* ("thence [from heaven] [he] will come to judge the dead and the living").

He therefore used *juzgaetan* ("to judge") in the inessive, instead of the standard *juzgaetara / juzgatzera*, in the allative.*

It seems that the inessive was not universally used in the province of Araba. Julián García de Albeniz and Juan Bautista Gamiz used the allative, and Juan Pérez de Lazarraga used both the allative and the inessive. Today, the inessive is the only option in most of Bizkaia and in the south of the Deba Valley, while in the north of the Deba Valley and in the northeastern part of Bizkaia, in the Artibai region (around Ondarroa and Markina) the allative is used.

6 The indefinite pronouns formed with the conjunction *edo* ("or") attached to the interrogative pronouns (*nor* ["who"], *noren* ["of whom"], *nori* ["to whom"], etc.) are typically western Basque. They seem to have arisen in imitation of the common *edozein* ("anyone"). Landucci's dictionary has practically the complete series: *edonolan* ("anyway"), *edonon* ("anywhere"), *edonondi* ("from anywhere"), *edonorean* ("of anywhere"), *edonorusç* ("towards anywhere"), *edonox* ("at any time"), etc. These pronouns may not have been common throughout Araba. Juan Bautista Gamiz, for example, at the eastern end of the province, used the standard *nornay / nornaic* ("anyone").

7 The adverbial suffix *-to* also seems to have originated in Araba. Nowadays it is no longer productive and survives in only a few words, mainly in Bizkaia. The best-known examples are *ederto* ("superbly"), *polito* ("pleasantly"), and *txarto* ("badly"), as well as *ondo* ("well") and *hobeto* ("better"). These were widely distributed, across the whole of Gipuzkoa and the Navarrese region of Burunda. In at least some parts of Araba, adverbs with the suffix *-to* were more widely found in the past. In Juan Pérez de Lazarraga's work, it was even used to accompany words from Castilian: *cortesdo* ("courteously") and *cureldo* ("cruelly").

8 The tendency to add an *-n* to the adverbial suffix *-la* is another of the changes that may have originated in Araba. Landucci's dictionary, for example, has *beralan* ("indistinctly"), *bestelan* ("diversely"), *edonolan* ("whichever"), *nolan* ("how"), and *onelan* ("thus"). The phenomenon may not have covered the entire province of Araba and may have been more pronounced in some places than in others. Juan Pérez de Betolatza (1596) used the *-n*, for example, but Juan Pérez de Lazarraga ([2004] c. 1564) did not. Today, *-n* is used throughout Bizkaia and in some parts of the Deba Valley, but it is also used sporadically in other parts of the Basque Country. In Zuberoa, in the east, the *bestelan* variant occurs frequently, and it is customary to add *-n* to the morpheme of the comitative* *-kilan* (*lagünaekilan* ["with the friend"]), as well as to the loan *sekülan* ("never") (from the Latin *saeculum* ["century"]).

9 The use of the root *eutsi* in verbs of the absolute-dative-ergative type* is documented in texts from the eastern end of Araba. For example, the verses of Juan Bautista Gamiz (eighteenth century) have *esan dust* ("he has told to me"), *eraman duztazu* ("you have brought it to me"), and *eguingo duzco* ("will do it to us").

In the eastern region of Araba, the western root *eutsi* and the central *-i-* coexisted, as can be seen from the writings of Pérez de Lazarraga, García de Albeniz, and Gamiz himself. The same probably happened in the Deba Valley, to judge by the *Endechas de doña Milia de Lastur* ("Doña Milia de Lastur's laments"), collected by Esteban Garibai in the sixteenth century, and apparently composed in the previous century (Mitxelena 1964: 75–79). Subsequently, however, the *eutsi* root became the only option in Bizkaia and most of the Deba Valley, just as it was in the catechism of the Araban Juan Pérez de Betolatza (1596).

10 In verbs of the absolutive-dative type,* there has been a special phonetic evolution in the western dialect, which has *j-* instead of the usual *z-*. Thus, Juan Pérez de Lazarraga has *jat* ("is to me") (cf. *zait*), *jaçu* ("is to you") (cf. *zaizu*), *jacu* ("is to us") (cf. *zaigu*), *nachaçu* ("I am to you") (cf. *natzaizu*), and *jacan* ("was to him/her") (cf. *zitzaion*).

In the Navarrese region of Burunda, bordering on Araba, verbal inflections of the familiar type currently occur whose absolutive* morpheme is the western *j-*: *jituet* ("I have them") (cf. *ditiat*), *jeat* ("I have to him/her") (cf. *zioat*), *jukat* ("I have it") (cf. *zaukaat*), *jakiai* ("they know it") (cf. *zakitek*), *jok* ("is") (cf. *zagok*), and *jeilek* ("goes") (cf. *zabilek*). Presumably this special phonetic evolution extended to Bizkaia, the Deba Valley, and Burunda, starting from Araba.

11 We saw in the previous chapter how Basque has many ways of forming verb plurals. The Western dialect has a practically unique one, *-z*, which is added to the end of the verbal inflection. The same option is already present in texts from Araba. Juan Pérez de Lazarraga provides several examples, including *daoz* ("they are") (cf. *daude*), but the most characteristic is *çaitudaz* ("I to you") (cf. *zaitut*), a pleonastic form, where in addition to the standard morpheme *-it-* we have the western *-z*. Juan Pérez de Betolatza has a similar example: *dituz* ("has them") (cf. *ditu*).

12 As Blanca Urgell (2006: 933) has pointed out, the suffix of the verbal noun *-etan* (> *-itan*) may have originated in Araba. In Landucci's dictionary, it is used with verbs ending in *-adu*, *-atu*, *-idu*, and *-e*: *confiaytan* ("trusting") (standard *konfiatzen*), *escaytan* ("requesting") (cf. *eskatzen*), *desfavoreçietan* ("disfavouring") (cf. *desfaborezitzen*), and *gordaytan* ("guarding") (cf. *gordetzen*). This suffix is currently used in most of Bizkaia and in the southern part of the Deba Valley.

In the Western dialect, there are other options for constructing the verbal noun, and it is likely that the following two (at least) came originally from Araba. On the one hand, *-ketan*, a variant of the previous *-etan*, comonly used with verbs of more than two syllables ending in *-tu:*

aguinquetan ("ordering") (cf. *agintzen*). And, on the other hand, *-zaiten*, used with verbs of two syllables ending in *-tu: arçayten* ("taking it") (cf. *hartzen*). Both examples are from Landucci's dictionary.

The first of the two suffixes (*-ketan*) is currently used in the southern part of the Deba basin, bordering on Araba, in Oñati, Aramaio, and the Leintz Valley. As for *-zaiten*, it no longer survives in present-day Basque, but was at one point known in some parts of Bizkaia, for example, around Bilbao. In the work of Rafael Mikoleta (1653) we find *galsayten* ("losing") and *sarsayten* ("entering").

13   Finally, it is possible that the suffix *-terren* (> *-tearren*, currently), used in causal and final sentences, might have arisen in Araba. It brings together two general Basque morphemes: *-te*, characteristic of the verbal noun (*ikuste* ["the seeing"]), and *arren*, in concessive sentences (*ikusi arren* ["although I see it"]). The following example is from Juan Pérez de Lazarraga: *ene lagunau eta ni goaç ara, Silveroren jentilezac ecusterren* ("my friend and I go there, to see the kindnesses of Silvero"). Here, we have *ecusterren* ("[in order] to see").

Central Bizkaia

Bizkaia's innovative nuclei

I already mentioned in the previous section that Bizkaia's biggest centres of population in ancient times were on the slopes of the Oiz and Sollube mountains (García Camino 2002). These were probably the foci whence Bizkaia's main linguistic innovations emanated – more specifically, from the axis formed around Durango, Amorebieta, Gernika, and Bermeo, places located along an important communications route that joined Gasteiz to the coast.

Bilbao itself does not seem to have played much of a role in the formation of the Bizkaian dialect. Its growth was belated, after the fourteenth century, by which time the western dialect had already shaped up and consolidated. Given the slow pace at which linguistic fashions spread in past times, we must assume that its origin dated back several centuries.

On the other hand, by the time that Bizkaian Basque began to be used in literature (the start of the nineteenth century), Bilbao was already highly Castilianised. Larramendi (1745: xxviii) makes no bones about it:

> Although in Bilbao people speak poorly, it is not so on the outskirts, where propriety and pronunciation are well preserved, and the same would be the case in Bilbao itself if they were more proud of being Basque: nor do I want to say that there is no one in Bilbao who knows his dialect well, for there are some.[1]

Larramendi was talking about Bilbao in the mid-eighteenth century, so the deterioration of Basque must have started well before that time. In the early nineteenth century, Juan Antonio Mogel (1987 [Villasante, ed.]: 90) described the state of Basque in Bilbao:

> [In Bilbao], it seems they take pains to make a *tercium quid* out of Castilian and Basque.[2]

So, it seem that Bilbao played little or no role in the formation of the Bizkaian dialect, despite the arguments put forward by Blanca Urgell (2006: 945).

Some of the innovations that I consider properly Bizkaian are undoubtedly ancient, but others seem more modern, and probably postdate the nineteenth century. I have not found any evidence of them in old documents I have consulted.

Ancient innovations

1   The Bizkaian variant *-txu* of the diminutive suffix (cf. standard *-txo*) appeared in a letter written by the Duranguese bishop Fray Juan de Zumarraga in 1537 (Sarasola 1983: 97–102). It contains the words *calderetachu bat* ("a small caldron"). The same suffix appears in Rafael Mikoleta's manuscript, written on the dialect's western edge, where the following Castilian words are translated into Basque:

> *un çerçeganillo* ("fresh air"): *axechu ozbat*
> *un sonito de chapin* ("light sound of footwear"): *chapinen oschubat*
> *por esta ondilla* ("by this deep cup"): *saconchu onetati*

   But the *-txu* variant has also been used in Araba, for example in the name *Txagorritxu* (<*etxe gorritxo*) ("little red house"), a well-known quarter in Gasteiz.

2   In Bizkaian Basque, in synthetic forms of the verb *esan* ("to say"), with the root *-io-*, an *-n-* is intercalated, so that the root turns into *-iño*. For example, Mikoleta has *diñot* ("I say"), *diño* ("he/she says"), *diñoe* ("they say"), *diñosu* ("you [polite] say"), *diñoda* ("that I say") (cf. *diot, dio, diote, diozu, diodan*).

3   Bizkaian also adds the morpheme *-ten* of the verbal noun to the suffix *-tu* of the participle. Mikoleta often uses these verbal nouns ending in *-tuten:* *adituten* ("looking") (cf. *aditzen*), *aguinduten* ("ordering") (cf. *agintzen*), *astuten* ("forgetting") (cf. *ahazten*), *biortuten* ("returning") (cf. *bihurtzen*), *elduteco* ("in order to arrive") (cf. *heltzeko*), and *gogaytuten* ("angering") (cf. *gogaitzen*). However, such constructions can also be found sporadically in other dialect areas.

4   In Bizkaia and most of the Deba Valley, it is practically a rule to put the demonstrative before the noun. The earliest evidence I have found of this tendency is in a seventeenth-century catechism whose author and place of origin are unknown (Mitxelena 1954: 92 and 93):

onec circumstancie bioc ("these two circumstances")
oneec amar mandamientuoc ("these ten commandments")

In the other dialects, one would say *bi zirkunstanzia* hauek and *hamar mandamiento hauek.*

More recent innovations

The innovations I discuss here are generally limited to Bizkaia. They have not got as far as the Deba Valley and have not even reached the Artibai region (the Ondarroa and Markina area), at the northeastern tip of the province. Nor are they always observed in other lateral dialects of Bizkaia. Here I list four innovations:

1   The diphthong *-au-* tends to become *-eu-*: *eurre* ("in front") (cf. standard *aurre), geur* ("today") (cf. *gaur), geuza* ("thing") (cf. *gauza*), and *jeusi* ("to fall") (cf. *jausi*). It is particularly frequent in participles ending in *-au: konteu* ("counted") (cf. *kontatu), paseu* ("passed") (cf. *pasatu*), etc.
     In the inflections of the verb "to have" the process has gone one step further, from *-eu-* to *-e-: dekot* ("I have"), *dekozu* ("you have"), *deko* ("he/she has"), *dekogu* ("we have"), etc. (cf. *daukat, daukazu, dauka, daukagu*).

2   The vowel *i* has palatalised the consonant *z* that follows it, thus turning it into *x: bixer* ("beard") (cf. standard *bizar), bixi* ("to live") (cf. *bizi), gixon* ("man") (cf. *gizon), ixera* ("sheet") (cf. *izara), dakixu* ("you know") (cf. *dakizu*), etc. In the western region, this innovation has been in existence for a very long time, but only after semivocal *j: axe* ("wind") (cf. *haize*).

3   Indefinite pronouns with the structure interrogative pronoun + *edo* + interrogative pronoun are typically Bizkaian: *nor edo nor* (> *nonor*) ("someone"), *nor edo nori* (> *nonori*) ("to someone"), *nor edo nogaz* (> *nonogaz*) ("with someone"), etc. Some are known outside Bizkaia, in particular *zer edo zer* (> *zeozer*) ("something"), which is general in Gipuzkoa and the western districts of Navarre.

4   The verbal pluraliser *-z* has displaced all the other options in Bizkaia. It occurs even in the inflections of the auxiliary "to have": *dauz* ("has them") (cf. standard *ditu), nebazan* ("I had them") (cf. *nituen), ebazan* ("he/she had them") (cf. *zituen*), etc. In the inflections of the auxiliary "to be" *-z* is often used redundantly: *direz* ("they are") (cf. *dira), zintzezan* ("you were") (cf. *zinen), gintzezan* ("we were") (cf. *ginen*), etc.

Zuberoa and Lower Navarre

A significant number of linguistic changes have taken place in the eastern part of the Basque Country. Their boundaries often coincide with and generally embrace the provinces of Zuberoa, Lower Navarre, and the eastern part of Lapurdi. They also stretch as far as the valleys of the northeastern part of

Navarre – Erronkari, Zaraitzu, and sometimes Aezkoa. It is not clear where the radiating focus lies. However, given their precise spread, it is necessary to rule out Lapurdi. One must also rule out the Navarrese valleys mentioned above, given their low economic and demographic potential. All that remains would seem to be Zuberoa and Lower Navarre, or – more specifically – their main urban centres: Maule (Mauleon) and Atharratze (Tardets), in Zuberoa, and Donibane Garazi (Saint-Jean-Pie-de-Port) and Donapaleu (Saint-Palais), in Lower Navarre. However, the radiating focus might have lain outside the present Basque Country, in Béarn or Huesca, for example.

In this section, a distinction is drawn between two groups of innovations: those that have extended along the lines indicated above, and those that, starting probably from Zuberoa, are recorded in Zuberoa and in some neighbouring speech communities, mainly in Navarre's Erronkari Valley.

Innovations in the eastern region

1   The vowel *u*, joined to *a* or *e*, yields *i: eskia* ("the hand") (cf. standard *eskua*) and *diela* ("that has") (cf. *duela*). However, in an earlier phase the result was *-uya / -uye*, as in the poems published in 1545 by Etxepare (1545: I: 48):

> *graciac oro vere escuyan nahi duyen orduyan* ("all the graces in his hand, at the instant that he desires")

Hence, *escuyan* ("in the hand") (cf. *eskuan),* *duyen* ("in which") (cf. *duen*), and *orduyan* ("in the instant") (cf. *orduan*).

2   In the inflections both of auxiliary verbs of the absolutive* type and of the absolutive-ergative* type, two diphthong reductions occur. In the first, *-ai-* becomes *-i-*; in the second, *-au-* becomes *-u-*. In Etxepare's poetry, the passage from *-ai-> -i-* has already happened in the following verbal forms: *niz* ("I am"), *iz* ("you are"), *guitu* ("he has to us"), *guituçu* ("you have to us"), *citut* ("I have to you"), *guiçaque* ("he can to us") (cf. *naiz, haiz, gaitu, gaituzu, zaitut, gaitzake*). In these other ones, *-au-* has become *-u-*: *nuc* ("you have to me"), *nuçu* ("you [polite] have to me"), *nu* ("he/she has to me") (cf. *nauk, nauzu, nau*).

The reductions of *-ai-* to *-i-* and *-au-* to *-u-* are general (*orain* ["now"]> *oin, basaurde* ["wild boar"]> *basurde*, for example), but in the eastern region they are systematically produced in this type of verbs, with very few exceptions, such as the Roncalese verbal form *naz* ("I am") for *niz*.

3   The morpheme of the dative plural has the variant *-er* (standard *-ei*). Here is an example from Etxepare (1545: I: 53): *saynduyer ere eguin eçac heure eçagucia* ("also presents your recognition to the saints"). Thus, *saynduyer* ("to the saints") (cf. standard *santuei*).

4   The morpheme of the comitative* has the variant *-kila*, alongside *-ki* and the more general *-kin*. The poet Etxepare (1545: II: 63) writes: *harequila*

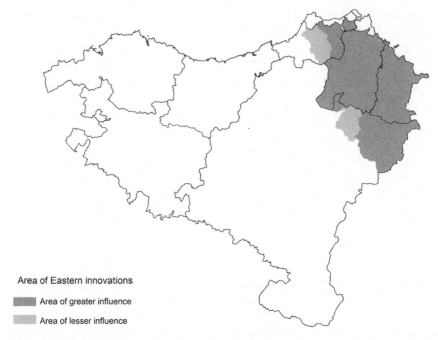

Area of Eastern innovations

███ Area of greater influence

░░░ Area of lesser influence

Figure 3.5 Area of eastern innovations

segur dugu vehar dugun gucia ("with him we have ensured everything we need"). Thus, *harequila* ("with him") (standard *harekin*).

5   The main innovation in the eastern area is undoubtedly the fact of having organised a complete verbal system, the *"zuka"* type, which is used as a mark of respect. These verbal inflections are present in the poems of Etxepare (1545), whence the following examples:

> *minzaceco çurequila gau bat nahi niqueci* ("I would like to have a night to talk with you") (VI: 15)
> *secretuqui vehar dicit harequila minçatu* ("I must speak with her in secret") (VII: 11)

The *niqueci* ("would like") and *dicit* ("I have") inflections replace the standard *nuke* and *dut*.

In a later period, a second innovation came about when these inflections were palatalised. For example, from *dizit* ("I have") the pronunciation *dixit* emerged. The area of this change is smaller than that of the previous one – it has been limited to most of Lower Navarre, the northeastern part of Lapurdi, and the Navarrese Zaraitzu Valley. Given its geography, the most likely place of origin of the innovation is Donibane Garazi (Saint-Jean-Pie-de-Port) and the surrounding region (on the use of the forms of treatment – respectful and familiar – in Basque, see Alberdi 1996).

6   The interrogative suffix -*a*, which is already present in the work of Etxe-
     pare (1545):

> *beti ere vehar duta nic çugatic dolore* ("do I always have to suffer for
> you?") (VII: 2)
> *honeyn sarri vci nahi nuçuya* ("so soon do you wish to leave me?")
> (x: 10)

We find the suffix in the verbal inflections *duta* (<*dut* + *a*) ("do I have
it?") and *nuçuya* (<*nuzu* + *a*) ("do you have to me?").

Zuberoan innovations

These innovations seem to be typical of Zuberoa. Most have also been recorded
in Navarre's Erronkari Valley, which has maintained close relations with
Zuberoa. Other of the innovations have spread more widely, even to some places
in Lower Navarre and the Zaraitzu Valley. They are five in number:

1   When words ending in -*a* are joined to the article, the result has been -*a* + *a*>
     -*aa*> -*á*. It is typical of Zuberoa and Erronkari, but in ancient times it was
     more widespread. Joanes Leizarraga, for example, who had the good sense to
     use accent marks to indicate word-stress, shows that in his speech community
     the same outcome resulted. Leizarraga was originally from Beskoitze (Bris-
     cous), in the northeast of Lapurdi. His version of the New Testament contains
     the following passage, with two examples (1571: 25), *landá* ("the field") and
     uztá ("the harvest"): "*landá da mundua* [...] *eta uztá, munduaren fina* ("the field
     is the world and the harvest, the end of the world").
2   Two vowel assimilations are practically systematic in Zuberoa and Erronkari,
     u - *i* to *u* - *u* and, above all, *i* - *u* to *u* - *u*. In Zuberoa, later, *u* became *ü* under the
     influence of Occitan. There are numerous examples in the catechism of the
     Zuberoan priest Athanase Belapeyre, published in 1696, and one of the first
     texts written in that dialect: *bühürtü* ("to be converted") (cf. standard *bihurtu*),
     hügün ("disgusting") (cf. *higuin*), *ülhün* ("dark") (cf. *ilun*), and *üngürü*
     ("around") (cf. *inguru*). However, such assimilations occur sporadically
     throughout the Basque Country. For example, in Bizkaia, at the western end,
     burduntzi ("spit, roaster") and *burduntzali* ("saucepan"), whose first element is
     burdina ("iron"); and *guntzurrun* ("kidney") (cf. standard *giltzurdin*), *guzur*
     ("lie") (cf. *gezur*), and *urun* ("flour") (cf. *irin*).
3   In both Zuberoa and Erronkari, the diphthong -*au*- has been transformed
     into -*ai*- in certain contexts. Belapeyre's catechism has, for example,
     belhañ (<belhain) ("knee") (cf. standard *belaun*), *gai* ("night") (cf. *gau*),
     gaiza ("thing") (cf. *gauza*), *haitatü* ("choose") (cf. *hautatu*), *irain / irañ*
     ("to remain") (cf. *iraun*), etc.
4   The allative* suffix in Zuberoa is -*ala(t)*, with the article, in common
     words (cf. standard -*ra*). Cf. Belapeyre's catechism (Belapeyre 1696):

> *alde honiala* ("to the good side") (103)
> *bekhatiala ez erorteco* ("so as not to fall into sin") (127)

where we encounter *honiala* ("to the good") (cf. standard *onera*) and *bekhatiala* ("to the sin") (cf. *bekatura*). This change also spread to the Navarrese valleys of Zaraitzu and Erronkari.

5   The diminutive suffix *–ñi* is native to Zuberoa. Belapeyre's catechism has *amiñi* ("a little bit") and *ttipiñi* ("tiny").

Beterri

Beterri is that part of Gipuzkoa between Donostia-San Sebastián and Tolosa. It is on the major communications route that has, since ancient times, united Iruña with the Gipuzkoan coast, where, in addition to the two places already mentioned, there have been, also since ancient times, other important centres of population like Andoain and Hernani. Given the area to which certain linguistic phenomena apply, it seems to me that Beterri may also have been an innovative focus.

The degree to which it led or helped shape developments is easier to measure in more recent times. The first attempt to revitalise Basque in the southern Basque Country came in the mid-eighteenth century, and the Beterri region played a decisive role in it. The two chief architects, the Jesuits Larramendi and Kardaberatz, came from that area.

Of the oldest Gipuzkoan linguistic changes, I cite four:

1   The root *-e* in present-tense inflections of the auxiliary verb *edun* ("to have"): *det* ("I have"), *dek / den* ("you [singular] have"), *dezu* ("you [polite] have"), *degu* ("we have"), and *dezue* ("you [plural] have").

2   Special verbal inflections of the verb *joan* ("to go"): *nijoa* ("I go"), *dijoa* ("he/she goes"), *dijoaz* ("they go") (cf. standard *noa, doa, doaz*).

3   The root *-e-* in present inflections of the auxiliary verb *izan* ("to be"): *zera* ("you are"), *gera* ("we are"), *zerate* ("you [plural] are") (cf. *zara, gara, zarete*).

4   Use of the pluraliser *-zki-* in verbs of the absolutive-ergative type* in familiar treatment: *dizkiat / dizkinat* ("I have them"), *dizkik / dizkin* ("he/she has them"), *dizkiagu / dizkinagu* ("we have them"), *dizkiate / dizkinate* ("they have them") (cf. *ditiat / ditinat, ditik / ditin, ditiagu / ditinagu, ditiztek / ditizten*).

Conclusions

As I explained in the preceding chapter, the truly divergent dialects are those at each end of the country, Zuberoan and, in particular, the western dialect, of Araba, Bizkaia, and Gipuzkoa's Deba Valley. It is clear from this chapter that many innovations started out in these two places.

If that is indeed the case, it is necessary, in the first place, to deal with the view of Blanca Urgell (2006: 941), who calls the "linguistic east" conservative and archaising. It is true that many of the innovations that arose in the central region have not reached those places, or reached them only later, but that does not mean in any way that the eastern region has remained stationary and stagnant. I therefore think that it would be more appropriate to say that the East has followed "its own dynamic."

In the central region, in addition to the role played by Iruña in ancient times, the Beterri region of Gipuzkoa has also been innovative. As for Lapurdi, no significant innovative activity can be observed, but more attention must be paid to the influence exercised by writers in the seventeenth century on the Lapurdian coast. As Ibon Sarasola (1986) has pointed out, their creations in the field of lexicon and especially their diffusion of compound words and derivatives (for example) may have served as a point of reference for the writers in the other dialect areas.

I would like to emphasise that the cities were probably the main focus of linguistic innovation. These would include Iruña, first and foremost, then Gasteiz, and then Maule, Atharratze, Donibane Garazi, and Donapaleau, in the eastern area, located along the Tolosa–Donostia axis in Gipuzkoa and, probably, the Durango–Bermeo axis in Bizkaia.

But despite the advances made in recent times in Basque dialectology, the past and the evolution of the dialects are still little known, and as the research field grows and knowledge deepens, the findings presented in this book will be amplified and, in many cases, corrected and amended.

Notes

1 Aunque en Bilbao se habla mal, pero no es assi en sus cercanías, donde la propriedad y pronunciacion se conservan en su punto, y sucediera lo mismo en el mismo Bilbao, si en este punto se picaran algo mas de Bizcainos: ni en esto quiero decir, que no ay en Bilbao quien sepa bien su Dialecto, pues se hallan algunos.
2 No hablo de Bilbao, porque parece que aquí se esmeran en sacar un *tercium quid* de la lengua castellana y la bascongada.

References

Alberdi, Jabier. 1996. *Euskararen tratamenduak: erabilera*. Bilbao: Real Academia de la Lengua Vasca.
Altuna Otegi, Fidel. 1995. "Acto contriciocoa eriotzaco orduracò: Garcia de Albeniz araiarraren araberazko eskuizkribua (1778)". *Anuario del Seminario de Filología Vasca "Julio de Urquijo"*, 29–1: 83–132. Donostia: Diputación Foral de Gipuzkoa.
Altuna Otegi, Fidel. 2002. "Arabako euskal testu zahar gehiago: Gamarra eta Luzuriaga xvii. mendeko bi arabarren lekukotza". (X. Artiagoitia, P. Goenaga and J. A. Lakarra, eds.) *Erramu boneta: Festschrift for Rudolf P. G. de Rijk. Anejos del Anuario del Seminario de Filología Vasca "Julio de Urquijo"*, nº 44, 27–52. Bilbao: Universidad del País Vasco.
Añibarro, Pedro Antonio. 1969. *Gramática bascongada*. (L. Villasante, ed.) *Anuario del Seminario de Filología Vasca "Julio de Urquijo"*, 3: 3–169. Donostia: Diputación Foral de Gipuzkoa.

Azkarate, Agustín and José Luis Solaun. 2009. "Nacimiento y transformación de un asentamiento altomedieval en un futuro centro de poder: *Gasteiz* desde fines del siglo VII d. C. a inicios del segundo milenio". (J. A. Quirós Castillo, ed.) *The archaeology of early medieval villages in Europe*: 405–425. Leioa: Universidad del País Vasco.

Barandiaran, José Miguel. 1973. *Obras completas* (II). Bilbao: La Gran Enciclopedia Vasca.

Barrena, Elena. 1989. *La formación histórica de Guipúzcoa*. Donostia: Cuadernos Universitarios, Sección Historia, nº 5, E.U.T.G.- Mundaiz.

Belapeyre, Athanase. 1696. *Catechima laburra eta Jesus Christ goure ginco jaunaren eçagutcia, salvatu içateco*. Pau: Jerôme Dupoux. Reprinted in (J. L. Davant, ed.) Bilbao: Real Academia de la Lengua Vasca, 1983.

Beriain, Juan. 1621. *Tratado de como se ha de oyr missa, escrito en Romance, y Bascuence, lenguages de este Obispado de Pamplona*. Facsimile: Donostia, Hordago, 1980.

Bonaparte, Louis-Lucien. 1867. *Observations sur le formulaire de prône conservé naguère dans l'église d'Arbonne*. London.

Carrera, Ignacio M. and Imanol García. 2005. *Legutiano aldeko euskara*. Gasteiz: Diputación Foral de Araba.

Etxepare, Bernat. 1545. *Linguae Vasconum Primitiae*. (P. Altuna, ed.) Bilbao: Mensajero, 1980.

García Camino, Iñaki. 2002. *Arqueología y poblamiento en Bizkaia, siglos VI-XII: La configuración de la sociedad feudal*. Bilbao: Diputación Foral de Bizkaia.

García-Gómez, Ismael. 2017. *Vitoria-Gasteiz y su hinterland. Evolución de un sistema urbano entre los siglos XI y XV*. Leioa: Universidad del País Vasco.

Goikoetxea, Jon. 1984. *Juan Bautista Gamiz Ruiz de Oteo, poeta bilingüe alavés del siglo XVIII*. Gasteiz: Diputación Foral de Araba.

González Salazar, José Antonio. 1985–1998. *Cuadernos de toponimia* (8 vols). Gasteiz: Diputación Foral de Araba.

Knörr, Henrike. 1998. "Euskal-erdal eguberri kanta (1695)". (H. Knörr and K. Zuazo, eds.) *El euskara alavés. Estudios y textos*: 503–510. Gasteiz: Parlamento Vasco.

Knörr, Henrike. 2005. "Zigoitiko aditza (1918)", *Nerekin yaio nun. Txillardegiri omenaldia*: 315–338. Bilbao: Euskaltzaindia.

Landucci, Niccolò, 1562. *Dictionarium linguae cantabricae*. Reprinted in (H. Knörr and K. Zuazo, eds.) *El euskara alavés. Estudios y textos*: 201–465. Gasteiz: Parlamento Vasco, 1998.

Larramendi, Manuel. 1729. *El impossible vencido. Arte de la Lengua Bascongada*. Salamanca: Antonio Joseph Villagordo Alcaráz.

Larramendi, Manuel. 1745. *Diccionario trilingüe del castellano, bascuence y latín*. Donostia: Bartolomé Riesgo y Montero.

Larramendi, Manuel. 1969. *Corografía o descripción general de la muy noble y muy leal provincia de Guipúzcoa*. (J. I. Tellechea Idigoras, ed.) Donostia: Sociedad Guipuzcoana de Ediciones y Publicaciones.

Larrea, Juan José. 1996. "El obispado de Pamplona en época visigoda". *Hispania Sacra*, 48: 123–147. Madrid: Consejo Superior de Investigaciones Científicas.

Leizarraga, Joanes. 1571. *Jesus Christ gure Jaunaren Testamendu Berria*. La Rochelle: Pierre Hautin. Facsímil: Donostia, Hordago, 1979.

López de Guereñu, Gerardo. 1989. *Toponimia alavesa, seguido de mortuorios o despoblados y pueblos alaveses*. Bilbao: Real Academia de la Lengua Vasca.

López de Guereñu, Gerardo. 1998. *Voces alavesas.* Bilbao: Real Academia de la Lengua Vasca.

Merino Urrutia, José J. Bautista. 1978. *La lengua vasca en La Rioja y Burgos.* Logroño: Servicio de Cultura de la Excma. Diputación Provincial de Logroño.

Mikoleta, Rafael. 1653. *Modo breve de aprender la lengua vizcayna.* Reprinted in (A. Zelaieta, ed.) Bilbao: AEK, 1995.

Mitxelena, Koldo. 1954. "Un catecismo vizcaíno del siglo xvii". *Boletín de la Real Sociedad Vascongada de los Amigos del País*, 10: 85–95. Donostia: Diputación Foral de Gipuzkoa.

Mitxelena, Koldo. 1964. *Textos arcaicos vascos.* Reprinted in *Anejos del Anuario del Seminario de Filología Vasca "Julio de Urquijo"*, nº 11. Donostia: Diputación Foral de Gipuzkoa and Universidad del País Vasco, 1990.

Mogel, Juan Antonio. 1987. *Cristaubaren icasbidea edo doctrina cristiania.* (L. Villasante, ed.) Bilbao: Real Academia de la Lengua Vasca.

Monteano, Peio J. 2017. *El iceberg navarro. Euskera y castellano en la Navarra del siglo xvi.* Iruña: Pamiela.

Oihenart, Arnaut. 1656. *Notitia utriusque Vasconiae tum Ibericae tum Aquitanicae.* Second revised edition. Translated by Javier Gorosterratzu. *Revista Internacional de Estudios Vascos*, 17–19. Bilbao: La Gran Enciclopedia Vasca, 1971–1972.

Ormaetxea, José Luis. 2006. *Aramaioko euskara (Azterketa dialektologikoa).* Bilbao: Universidad del País Vasco.

Pérez de Betolatza, Juan. 1596. *Doctrina Christiana.* Reprinted in (J. A. Arana Martija, ed.) *Euskera*, 31–2: 505–526. Bilbao: Real Academia de la Lengua Vasca, 1986.

Pérez de Lazarraga, Juan. 2004. *Eskuizkribua.* Madrid: Edilán-Ars Libris and Diputación Foral de Gipuzkoa.

Pujana, Pedro. 1979. *El verbo vasco de Oleta (Araba).* Gasteiz: Diputación Foral de Araba.

Sarasola, Ibon. 1983. "Contribución al estudio y edición de textos antiguos vascos". Reprinted in *Anejos del Anuario del Seminario de Filología Vasca "Julio de Urquijo"*, nº 11. Donostia: Diputación Foral de Gipuzkoa and Universidad del País Vasco, 1990.

Sarasola, Ibon. 1986. "Larramendiren eraginaz eta". *Anuario del Seminario de Filología Vasca "Julio de Urquijo"*, 20–1: 203–215. Donostia: Diputación Foral de Gipuzkoa.

Urgell, Blanca. 2006. "Para la historia del sustantivo verbal en vasco". *Anuario del Seminario de Filología Vasca "Julio de Urquijo"*, 40/1–2: 921–948. Donostia and Bilbao: Diputación Foral de Gipuzkoa and Universidad del País Vasco.

Zuazo, Koldo. 2013. *The Dialects of Basque.* [Translated by Aritz Branton] Reno, Nevada: Center for Basque Studies.

Zuazo, Koldo. 2014. *Euskalkiak.* Donostia: Elkar.

4 Basque ideas about the dialects and attitudes towards them

I have pointed out that the division of Basque into dialects was an established fact as early as the sixteenth century. By then, speakers were themselves aware of it. What is surprising is that people viewed dialects in completely different ways in different periods.

In the beginning, throughout the sixteenth, seventeenth, and the first half of the eighteenth centuries, dialects were considered a problem, in that they hampered communication. On the other hand, their existence was explained as a consequence of the sorry state of the language.

Attitudes changed after the publication, in 1745, of Manuel Larramendi's *Diccionario trilingüe* (Trilingual dictionary; Larramendi 1745). From then onwards, the dialects were seen as a source of enrichment, as a treasure to be safeguarded and protected. This way of thinking is still deeply rooted today. However, around the middle of the twentieth century, an important group of people, in and around Bilbao, began to defend a contrary thesis: that the dialects were a veritable scourge, that they jeopardised the survival of the language, and that they were an impediment to adapting Basque to the needs of modern life.

The dialects up until 1745

For the Protestant priest Joanes Leizarraga, who translated the New Testament into Basque in the sixteenth century, the dialects were a headache that added greatly to the problems that he faced in his work. He said in the prologue (Leizarraga 1571):

> The diversity in the way of speaking in the Basque Country is well known, and it varies almost from house to house.[1]

Leizarraga's comment is very brief, but other testimonies from the period can help to deepen our understanding of the reasons for and consequences of the division of the language. The sixteenth century historian Esteban Garibai (1533–1599) identified two causes: the lack of grammar books and the fact of being in contact with two different languages, as a result of the administrative division of the Basque Country between the Kingdoms of France and Spain (Urkijo 1919 [1976]: 553–554):

> This language, like the other vulgar tongues not conserved in Art [i.e., grammar], is so depraved that if today people from the last few centuries were to be brought back to life, they would find it practically impossible to understand us, and we them, in the way someone from Bilbao understands another from Baiona only with the greatest difficulty, although both towns speak this language, in Bilbao with a huge admixture of Castilian and in Baiona with a no smaller admixture of French.[2]

The administrative division and the influence of two different languages in each part of the Basque Country was unanimously accepted by Basque writers of the time as the main reason for the division of the language. For example, in his prologue to *Guero*, Axular (1556–1644), a Navarrese by origin but living in Lapurdi, on the other side of the administrative border, wrote (Axular 1643: 17):

> I know that I cannot embrace all the ways of speaking, since in the Basque Country they are many and varied: in Navarre, Lower Navarre, Zuberoa, Lapurdi, Bizkaia, Gipuzkoa, Araba, and many other places. Not all Basques have the same laws and customs, or the same language, because they belong to different kingdoms.[3]

Another writer from Lapurdi, Joanes Etxeberri (1668–1749), echoed the same opinion at the beginning of the eighteenth century (Urkijo 1907 [1976]: 137):

> Since the Basques belong to different kingdoms, it is no surprise that there are variations in their ways of speaking. Those in some regions have relations with one of these kingdoms, while those of the other with the other, and from that relationship each borrows from a different foreign language, and that is the origin of the divergences, which in the long term will result in the extinction of the language.[4]

Here, I draw attention to an issue that worried a writer born outside the Basque Country, Esteve Materra. Materra noted the blind adherence of Basques to their own dialect, as well as a deep animosity towards the dialects of others. He wrote in the prologue to his *Dotrina christiana* (Christian doctrine; Materra 1617):

> I know that in the Basque Country people speak in many different ways, and everyone believes that the Basque language of his or her own locality is the best and the most beautiful. I suppose, for that reason, that the Basque I use will displease more than one group of people. However, I want you to know that I learned my Basque in Sara [a place in the

province of Lapurdi], and if I speak Lapurdian Basque well, you have no cause to curse me and despise me, since I know no other Basque than that. In any case, I do not intend to judge whether the Basque of Sara is the best and the purest; everyone can have their own opinion. And whoever is not at ease with this Basque of mine should write better in a better Basque, and it will not bother me or make me jealous.[5]

The administrative fragmentation of the Basque Country

Ever since the sixteenth century, the Basque Country has been divided between the kingdoms of France and Spain, each of which imposed its own language as the sole official language in the territory it controlled. This was, in the opinion of sixteenth- and seventeenth-century writers, the main cause of dialectal diversity in the Basque Country.

Within France and Spain, other subdivisions also played a role. In France, the province of Zuberoa was segregated from those of Lapurdi and Lower Navarre and united with part of Béarn. Administratively and ecclesiastically, Zuberoa depended, and continues to depend, on Oloron, a place in Béarn. In Spain the same applied: Navarre was viewed and treated differently from the other three Basque-speaking regions. Needless to say, these circumstances had an impact on the language.

The administrative structuring – or, to be more precise, destructuring – to which I refer probably explains a curious event in the local administration of the town of Urruña (Lapurdi), in 1680. As a result of litigation between it and the neighbouring Gipuzkoans of Hondarribia, letters were exchanged between the two municipalities. The correspondence began in Basque, but soon the officials in Urruña asked those in Hondarribia to write in Castilian.

The request cannot have been due to a difference in dialect, since Urruña and Hondarribia border on one another. A more likely explanation is that one belonged to France and the other to Spain: each employed a different spelling system, each borrowed words and terms from a different language, and each had adapted to a different and distinct culture. So even in the seventeenth century, these fissiparous tendencies were at work. Here is a fragment from the letter sent by the town council in Urruña (Mujika 1908 [1969]: 730):

> Since our languages are very different, we have great difficulty in understanding your letter. We would therefore like you to write to us in Castilian, and we will write back in French or Basque.[6]

Such behaviour became ever more common with the passage of time, as French and Castilian continued to gain ground. Basque, on the other hand, constantly yielded ground and, in the end, was used, more or less, only within the framework of each administrative district.

Dialect rivalries

I pointed out in Chapter 1 that Basque may have survived, among other reasons, because of the importance that Basques accord their language. But it seems that it was not only Basque in general that mattered but also its local forms, the speech of each community. The Frenchman Materra did not flinch from noting the adverse effect of such a fervent attachment, as early as 1617.

Curiously, a few years later, Axular repeated Materra's comment almost word for word, indicating that the problem was indeed real (Axular 1643: 18–19):

> Usually, both at the time of writing and the moment of speaking, every-one seems to think that his or her dialect is the best and the most beau-tiful. Therefore, although mine is not like yours, do not despise or reject it, and if you do not like my manner of speaking, speak in your own way, in accordance with what is in fashion in your own locality, so that I don't get angry or annoyed.[7]

This was one of the main problems Manuel Larramendi (1690–1766) faced in the eighteenth century. This Gipuzkoan Jesuit was the author of the first ever published Basque grammar, which he called, significantly, *El impossible vencido: Arte de la lengua bascongada* (The impossible defeated: Art of the Basque lan-guage). It appeared in 1729, and in it Larramendi wrote (Larramendi 1729: 14):

> It happens that many Basques only find the dialects of their own province good and elegant, a common disease of those who speak any language. [...] But it is a disease of passion, which must be cured with two ounces of reason and intelligence.[8]

In his *Corografía de Gipuzkoa*, he reflected in similar vein (Larramendi 1969 [Tellechea Idigoras, ed.]: 295):

> The dialect of Zuberoa, especially when spoken, is strong and manly; and if for this reason the Lapurdians call it rough, they respond by calling Lapurdian effeminate and finical; one dialect is always grumbling about another, with scant discretion.[9]

Larramendi was also the author, in 1745, of the first published Basque dictionary. It was then that this dialectal frenzy struck him in its true dimensions. His wish, from a logical point of view, was to place each Basque word, dialectal or not, alongside the corresponding Castilian word. But the problem was, as Larramendi soon found out, that Basques accep-ted only the words from their own dialects, rejecting the rest out of hand. To stop this happening, he gathered together all the Basque words but without specifying to which dialect each belonged. He explained his motives (Larramendi 1745: XLVI–XLVII):

In lumping everything together, I encounter an almost insuperable difficulty, which every Basque will naturally own. It is the opposition with which those of any given dialect are born in respect of other dialects, especially in regard to language, in which they insult and despise one another to a ridiculous degree, beyond all reason. [...] Although everyone knows, for example, that *dongea* and *gaistoa* both mean "bad," a Bizkaian would never want to use *gaistoa*, nor a Gipuzkoan *dongea*.[10]

The German linguist Wilhelm von Humboldt (1767–1835) echoed these rivalries on his trips to the Basque Country in the eighteenth and nineteenth centuries. He wrote about it in several of his works, including *Prüfung der Untersuchungen über die Urbewohner Hispaniens vermittelst der vaskischen Sprache* (Research into the primitive inhabitants of Spain through the Basque language), where he said (Humboldt 1958 [1821]: 207):

As I also often heard in the country, the dialects of the places most remote from one another are more similar in some of the words they use [...] than the closest ones, which repel each other because of jealousy born of proximity.[11]

The Bizkaian Franciscan José Antonio Uriarte (1812–1869) dealt with the same question in a letter to Prince Bonaparte in August 1857 (Ruiz de Larrinaga 1954: 252):

In Basque it is not possible to write to the taste of all. Not only each dialect but even each minor administrative region has its favoured idioms and terms, which it prefers above all others, even though it knows that they are better.[12]

So, the problem has long existed, and various solutions have been advanced in attempts to remedy it. Xabier Munibe (1723–1785), a native of Azkoitia (Gipuzkoa), opted for the following, when he wrote his opera *El borracho burlado* (Munibe 1764 [1991]: 204):

At first I planned to do the whole opera in Basque, but then I came across the problem of which dialect to use. If I had used the dialect of Azkoitia, the rest of the country up to the French border would not have thanked me, for they dislike the [Gipuzkoan] Basque or dialect of Goierri, and if I had used the dialect of Tolosa, Hernani, Donostia, etc., I would have exposed the actors to ridicule, for it would have been hard to imitate it well. For that reason, I had to content myself with reserving the Basque language for the sung parts, and doing everything else in Castilian.[13]

It was probably not just dialect rivalry that led Munibe to write his opera in Castilian but the lack of a true conviction that it could be done in

Basque. Remember what Larramendi said at the time – the wealthy classes in the Basque Country used Castilian, while Basque was seen as the language of villagers and of the poor and the illiterate. Munibe, Count of Peñaflorida, and one of the founders in 1764 of the Basque Society of the Friends of the Country, had not altogether managed to overcome this problem. That was perhaps why he had shielded himself behind the pseudonym Sister María de la Misericordia when, some years before, he had published a collection of Christmas carols in Basque, titled *Gavon sariac* (Christmas presents; Munibe 1762).

The change of discourse with Larramendi

In Chapter 1, I looked at Larramendi's vision of the state of Basque in the mid-eighteenth century: a language absolutely despised and marginalised. In Spain, people particularly looked down on it and, even within Basque provinces included in the Spanish state, Basques of a certain economic and cultural standing looked down upon it and refused to use it. Two passages in Larramendi's dictionary support this conclusion (Larramendi 1745: LIV):

> The first objection was to tell us that Basque is a barbaric language, incapable of culture, alien to method and art [i.e., grammar], a rough and intractable language.
> [...] The Basques do not seem to have esteemed it, or at least they have not manifested their esteem. They leave their country, they make as if they have forgotten it, they don't write it, they don't even want to write a letter in their own language.[14]

Larramendi's aim was to make Basque once more prestigious, so that it could be used in all those domains that a language needs in order to survive. He turned to an ancient and well-known argument: that Basque was a "matrix" language, one of the 72 languages that God created in the Babelian chaos. After that, it had been transferred to Spain: Basque was, in short, the first and only language that in ancient times had been spoken throughout the Iberian Peninsula. Subsequently, as a result of invasions by people of different languages and cultures, the races had mixed and only the shield of the Pyrenees had enabled the pure and uncontaminated Spaniards, that is, the present-day "Basques," to hold their own. So, the Basque language deserved every respect, and the descendants of those primitive settlers of Spain should use it with the utmost pride and honour (Tovar, 1980). On the other hand, given that Basque was a language of divine nature, it represented all kinds of virtues and perfections. Larramendi (1745) wrote as follows (XIV):

> And this is confirmed by the singular advantages of Basque, and the perfections of its structure, in which it overcomes all [other languages] and seems to yield to none: for indeed no man could be the author of such admirable harmony.[15]

However, the thesis of the universality of Basque in the Iberian Peninsula came up against a serious obstacle in the descriptions of geographers and historians of Roman times, who claimed to have found different peoples and languages at the time of their arrival in the Peninsula. To overcome this obstacle, Larramendi came up with a solution that would have fatal consequences: he argued that the "tongues" mentioned by those historians and geographers were, in fact, the dialects of Basque. Dialects which, being so different one from the other, had misled those who had no proper knowledge of the Basque language: Strabo, for example. In this way, an erroneous and harmful belief took shape: that the Basque dialects are so different and so varied that they can be considered as true "tongues." Larramendi (1745) said in this respect (CLVIII):

> Strabo speaks of Spain's native and maternal languages, and says that the Spanish did not use just one single vernacular and native language but many, but these were actually a host of dialects of the same Spanish language, common to all the Spanish provinces, which Strabo called different languages; in conclusion, Spanish language with its different dialects was Basque.
>
> (...)
>
> This mother tongue was Basque, which is a matrix tongue, and which even today has so many and such diverse dialects, and dialects so well ordered, and with such fixed roots, that one can with reason call them the *Bizkaian language, Gipuzkoan language, Araban language, Navarrese language*, and *Lapurdian language*, and yet they are nothing more than dialects of the same matrix tongue that we call Basque. Dialects so different that Gipuzkoans and Bizkaians can hardly understood each other, nor Lapurdians and Arabans, unless they have undertaken special study and reflection.[16]

It is interesting to compare these comments with what Larramendi had written in the grammar published a few years earlier. Then, he had seemed to think that the distances between dialects scarcely mattered. The contradiction is easy to explain: the grammar was intended for Basques who wanted to study and cultivate their language, while the prologue to the dictionary was aimed at Castilian speakers who saw Basque as a poor, savage, and deficient language. Here is what he said (Larramendi 1729: 12–13):

> Basque has a corpus of language common and universal to all its dialects. This Basque corpus includes all nouns and verbs considered separately, i. e., with their declinations and conjugations, and all the other parts of its sentences, all the infinitive modes, etc., in which there are no differences whatsoever. So the dialects are reduced to the declinations of nouns and pronouns, which consist of articles, and to the conjugations of the verb, which consist of different endings or inflections.[17]

Larramendi's dictionary prologue, on the other hand, has two whole chapters extolling the virtues and perfections of the dialects: Chapter Twelve, titled "Basque is delightful on account of the beautiful variety of its dialects," and Chapter Thirteen, titled "On the corpus of Basque, and whether it would be better, and more perfect, without the differences in dialects." Larramendi seems to be in apologetic mode, but whatever the case, the fact is that he failed altogether to convince the Spanish, though not to confuse the Basques. In fact, ever since then, people have believed that the dialects are very different from one another, as true "tongues," which in practice are mutually incomprehensible. On the other hand, the view has taken hold that these dialects are a source of enrichment for the language and should therefore be protected and cultivated.

The intervention by partisans of classic Lapurdian

Around 1950, pressed by the need for a standard language model, the Bizkaian Federico Krutwig (1921–1998) proposed adopting the Lapurdian dialect as the basis for such as project; more specifically, he proposed the language of Joanes Leizarraga, a sixteenth-century Lapurdian author (see, above all, Krutwig 1951, 1952, 1962 and Villasante 1952). In Krutwig's view, Leizarraga was one of the few Basque writers who had used a cultured register of the language, in his New Testament translation of 1571. Nearly all the other things that had been written in Basque and, of course, the dialects spoken at the time were, according to him, vulgar and deplorable, and useless and inadmissible as a basis on which to launch a project for the revitalisation of language.

One of Leizarraga's decisions that most appealed to Krutwig was to adopt Greek and Latin spelling in transcribing words taken from those languages: *philosophia*, for example, instead of *filosofía*. This, of course, was the spelling used by some of the most important European languages (German, French, or English, for example), but it had never caught on in the Basque Country. Not even Basque writers within the French state had adopted it, with the sole exception, of course, of Leizarraga.

Here are two fragments from an article published by Krutwig in 1951. In the first, it is clear that Krutwig rejects the language spoken by the Basques of the twentieth century and prefers Lapurdian authors of the sixteenth and seventeenth centuries (Krutwig 1951: 11):

> To carry out the unification of Basque, we must adopt the dialect that has been written the most, not the one that is spoken the most, for literary languages are by definition to be read. In our case it is classic Lapurdian, which has come down to us from Leizarraga, Axular, Etxeberri, and Haraneder.[18]

Here is Krutwig's argument regarding the use of Greco-Latin spelling (Krutwig 1951: 11):

Some people deem it appropriate to adapt the spelling of literary terms to the phonetic laws of Basque, on the grounds that it would be easier to use. This is wrong. Literary words should have the same physiognomy in all languages, Basque included. Culture is not for ordinary people. The lower ranks of society play no part in cultural issues.[19]

Krutwig's proposal got the backing of well-known figures in Basque cultural life. With one or two exceptions, they were all Bizkaians, and they included some members of the Academy of the Basque Language.

The appearance in 1964 of another proposal, based on the central dialect, dented the Krutwig model, and several of its supporters judged this new alternative model to be more realistic. Others aimed for a synthesis of the two proposals. The Bilbaoan Xabier Kintana was the leader of this trend, and counted on the support of the magazine *Anaitasuna*, where (in no. 226, January 1, 1972, on p. 16) the proposal for a joining together of the verbal systems of the Lapurdian and Gipuzkoan dialects as a means of attaining a standard Basque first saw light, in the face of majority opinion, which favoured the Gipuzkoan dialect to the exclusion of the rest.

The solution proposed by Kintana gave the language a wholly artificial air. Kintana's argument that the Gipuzkoan verb seemed to him to be ambiguous and defective was also unacceptable. As the linguist Koldo Mitxelena (following countless others) warned (Mitxelena 1972: 376–401), there are no languages or dialects that are in themselves more perfect and more precise than others. Mitxelena also pointed out that Kintana, in his reference to Gipuzkoan, was talking about the Basque dialect that had the most speakers and had been used in literature ever since the eighteenth century.

In short, the Kintana model, like that of Krutwig, failed to take into account the language spoken by twentieth-century Basques. This triggered three types of reaction. Some people, failing to understand this "modern" Basque, decided to abandon it and seek refuge in Castilian. In the eyes of others, from another sector of society, the project for a standard Basque was completely discredited. However, a large group of people, faced with the pressing need to adapt Basque to the demands of modern urban and industrial society, accepted the project without demur but also without evaluating the consequences that the decision to adopt it might have in future. The most serious consequence was that dialect varieties were left behind and even despised and ridiculed.

A rupture came about in the community of Basque speakers and its consequences were manifested, with especial virulence, in Bizkaia and particularly in Bilbao. There were not many Basque speakers in Bilbao in the early seventies, but even so two types of *ikastola* or Basque school, two types of *gau eskola* (adult evening classes), and two magazines, *Agur* and *Anaitasuna*, were created, the one in pure Bizkaian, the other in standard Basque heavily influenced by the Lapurdian dialect of the sixteenth and seventeenth centuries. In other places in Bizkaia, similar things happened. In Ondarroa, for example, two types of *ikastola* were set up, even though Ondarroa has fewer than ten thousand inhabitants.

From a contemporary perspective, it is hard to understand the rejection in Bizkaia of the project for a standard Basque, but it is veritably impossible to comprehend Krutwig and Kintana's proposal: the language they used seemed imported from another galaxy.

Speakers' perception of the distance between the dialects

Because of the troubled state of the Basque language and the myths that surrounded it, many Basques today believe that there are too many dialects and that the differences between them are insurmountable. Until recently, Basques speaking different dialects have tended to resort to a second language, French or Spanish, in order to communicate with one another. This has tended to happen, for example, during military service. Basques from different regions meet in the army, and French or Spanish have often been their main vehicles of communication.

The team set up by the Academy of the Basque Language to produce the linguistic atlas of Basque cited a case from Eugi, a town in the eastern part of Navarre, near the administrative border with France. A person interviewed told the researchers that the Zuberoan and Bizkaian dialects were absolutely incomprehensible to him (Euskaltzaindia 1999: 106):

> I have never been able to make myself understood when talking with the Bizkaians, never. They swallow their words, *tipttapttu* [...], like the Zuberoans in France. When I was in the army I had Bizkaian friends in my company, but I couldn't understand them, nor they me, so we went over to using Castilian.[20]

The following testimony was collected in Deba, a Gipuzkoan town close to Bizkaia (Txurruka and Urbieta 2003: 21):

> He was from Navarre, near the French border. He knew no Castilian, not a word, but we couldn't communicate in Basque either. The Bermeo dialect is also complicated, very closed. There were lots of Bizkaians, and there was one who didn't understand our Basque. He was from a small town, even further away than Bermeo. We understood his Basque fairly well, but he couldn't understand ours, and in the army he often spoke in Castilian, even though he knew Basque better, but he didn't understand [our Basque].[21]

The final testimony comes from Hondarribia (in Gipuzkoa). It is interesting because it is from the mouth of a sailor, a sector that until a few years ago was entirely Basque-speaking. However, the Bizkaian dialect from the

Bermeo area was unintelligible to the sailors from other areas too, and they communicated in Spanish (Sagarzazu 2005: 50):

> [Communication] in Basque is painful. Those of us who have been to sea have often been in Bizkaia, especially in the Bermeo area, and we had no choice but to speak Castilian.[22]

Without wanting in any way to disparage the value of these testimonies, it is necessary to point out that the same happens, more or less, in other languages. When speakers of different dialects come into contact for the first time, they often sound strange to one another, but usually the difficulties go away as relationships progress and deepen. Since the nineteenth century, what singles out Basque from many other European languages (as used in Europe) is the fact that some Basques have been bilingual and, when the slightest difficulty has arisen in communicating with other Basques, have been able to resort to French or Castilian. This has caused a certain degree of withering in the capacity of some Basque speakers to assimilate the rules and vocabulary of neighbouring dialects.

From a linguist's point of view, as I have already argued, there are only two dialects that have a well-defined personality, one at each end of the Basque Country: Zuberoan, on the one hand, and Western Basque, on the other. For the rest, the linguistic distances are relatively short between the central speech communities in the provinces of Gipuzkoa, Navarre, Lapurdi, and Lower Navarre. The main obstacle is the presence of French and Spanish, whose influence is increasing daily and affects all levels of language: phonology, morphology, syntax, and, of course, vocabulary. This is the main barrier between Gipuzkoa and Navarre, on the one hand, and Lapurdi and Lower Navarre, on the other.

We must certainly bear in mind that the special phonological rules observed in certain speech communities makes them difficult to understand at first contact. Examples of this are the dialects of northwestern Navarre, the regions of Bortziriak and Malerreka. Loss of vowels is habitual in them, as a result of which words are distorted in careless and colloquial conversation. For example, in the speech of Arantza (Bortziriak), *oinetakoak* ("footwear") is reduced to *óintkuk*, which when pronounced quickly and within a sentence is unintelligible for speakers of other areas.

The dialects of some coastal regions in Bizkaia, like Bermeo, Elantxobe, Lekeitio, or Ondarroa, are also somewhat idiosyncratic and distinct. This is perhaps in part because they have, to a certain extent, been isolated and enclosed within themselves. Their natural point of egress has been towards the sea, and their relations with surrounding places have been less frequent. They are relatively important centres of population, which has made it easier for them to be more or less linguistically self-sufficient.

Other regions that, due to their geographical position, have maintained contacts with a very diverse set of dialects also have numerous and salient distinctions. Probably the best example is the dialect of the valley of Burunda, located at the furthest edge of Navarre and bordering on Gipuzkoa and Araba. Until relatively recently, this region had a certain degree of administrative autonomy. More or less the same can be said of Irun, Hondarribia, and Oiartzun, which belong administratively to Gipuzkoa but maintain close relations with the provinces of Lapurdi and Navarre; and of the Navarrese valleys of Baztan, Aezkoa, Zaraitzu, and Erronkari, which have been in permanent contact with Basques on both sides of the Pyrenees.

Some reflections on the future

The origin and function of the dialects

Let us first do away with some myths about Basque and put things in their proper place. I have already indicated in Chapter 1 that the dialects are, to a large extent, a consequence of the problems that the Basque language community has suffered and continues to suffer: administrative fragmentation and, especially in Navarre and the northern provinces, social marginalisation. In addition, relations between Basques in different regions have historically, been few and generally weak. These are some of the main causes of Basque's dialectal diversification.

But we must not forget that the dialects are living remnants of the language, and that it is in these dialects that any attempt to recover the language must be based. It makes no sense to escape into the past and place the starting point in a period in which, so it might seem to us, the language was more splendid and glorious; in the Lapurdian dialect of the sixteenth and seventeenth centuries, for example. It would make even less sense to create a new language, without taking into account the current dialects.

In my opinion, the most sensible approach would be to take as one's base living Basque, to determine which are its most widespread and ingrained traits, and to use them to create the language of the future. On the other hand, in those places where Basque has been kept alive, the dialects must serve to enable the transmission of the language from parents to children, to which end the parents must value their language. If, to the contrary, they are given to understand that their dialects are degenerate and vulgar, it is highly unlikely that they will want to pass them on. This is the only conclusion to be drawn from the experiment carried out by the Bilbaoan "Lapurdianists" and, as we shall see later in this book, from other experiments of the same sort in the course of the twentieth century, which have had the same fatal consequences.

The distances between the dialects

Another myth that needs to dispelled is that the Basque dialects are completely different, to the point where they can better be considered as actual languages and where each is, practically speaking, unintelligible to speakers of other dialects, unless they have already learned them. This belief is absolutely false and, moreover, does the language great harm. If one adds to this belief the idea that Basque is an extremely difficult language – an idea also deeply rooted, both outside and inside the Basque Country – one ends up with a state of affairs in which people are actively discouraged from learning Basque.[23]

Here, I won't go into the question of whether Basque is simple or complicated, other than to remind readers of the universal principle that there are no languages that are, in and of themselves, either one thing or the other. The degree of ease or difficulty will depend on the language or languages that the learner already speaks. Since Basque is not an Indo-European language, it is not surprising that it strikes as strange speakers of languages that are, whether they be German, Italian, Catalan, or Gaelic. But if the learner is a speaker of a language belonging to any other language family, Basque will probably be no easier or harder than (say) Castilian (on this, see Moreno Cabrera 2007– 2008 and Moreno Cabrera 2000: 115–146).

Turning to the distances between the dialects, the most radical differences are a consequence of the administrative segregation of the Basque Country between France and Spain. Countless words used in daily life are different in French and Spanish, for example *alfombra/tapis* (carpet), *balance/bilan* (balance), *colchón/ matelas* (mattress), *cortina/rideau* (curtain), *limón/citron* (lemon), *pasear/promener* (walk), *pastel/gâteau* (cake), *postre/dessert* (desert), *presupuesto/budget* (budget), and *tortilla/omelette* (omelette). Some Basques use one form and others another, which often creates a muddle to which no satisfactory resolution has up to now been found.

In reality, however, the solution is readily to hand, in the common fund of Basque itself. To give some examples, the French conjunction *mais* (but) has always been *baina* in all dialects, so there is no need to borrow *mais* from French, as is often done. In the same way, it is not necessary to use the Castilian word *incluso* (even), given that at all times and in all dialects the Basques have used the word *baita* to express this concept. This is something that Basque speakers should also bear in mind, especially when it seems likely that the reader or listener comes from a different administrative region of the Basque Country.

The significance of the dialects for Basques

It is often said that there is an intimate relationship between the Basques and their dialects. They believe that they can see in their dialect an important part of their personality and that this has both a positive side and a negative side. This state of affairs can be viewed from three different angles:

1   This union has contributed to the ability of Basque to survive. It is therefore necessary to recognise that fact and to try to take advantage of it. As I said earlier, it is important not to engage in experiments that fail to take account of the reality of the dialects.
2   It is important that this union is seen in proper perspective, that one avoids falling into chauvinism and fanaticism, and that, in short, the language as a whole is taken into account and not just one's "own dialect."

3 I am particularly disturbed by the negative attitude some Basques strike towards people learning Standard Basque, whom they scorn or ridicule as speaking an "artificial" Basque, a "bookish" Basque, "unnatural" and without a "label of origin."

That some Basques prefer to speak French or Castilian with people who do not fully master Basque is particularly negative and harmful. The opposite should happen: one should speak Basque with learners, but calmly and patiently, avoiding contractions and attenuating, as far as possible, the use of local forms and terms.

But the main reason some Basque native speakers use French or Castilian with beginners or people who have learned the language as a second language is not that they feel contempt towards them but rather the opposite: they feel uncomfortable, since they are not properly literate in their native language and believe that it is they themselves who speak Basque poorly.

Notes

1 Batbederac daqui Heuscal Herrian quasi etche batetic bercera-ere minçatzeco manerán cer differentiá eta diversitatea den.
2 Esta lengua, la cual como las demás vulgares no conservadas en Arte, está depravada de tal manera, que si hoy resucitasen los de los siglos pasados de menos de mil años, no nos entendieran casi, ni nosotros a ellos, como hoy día se entienden con mucha dificultad el vecino de Bilbao y el de Bayona, con hablarse en ambos pueblos principales esta lengua, en Bilbao con muchísima mezcla de la castellana, y en Bayona con no menor de la francesa.
3 Badaquit halaber ecin heda naitequeyela euscaraco minçatce molde guztietara. Ceren anhitz moldez eta differentqui minçatcen baitira Euscal Herrian: Naffarroa garayan, Naffarroa beherean, Çuberoan, Laphurdin, Bizcayan, Gipuzkoan, Alaba herrian, eta bertce anhitz leccutan. (...) Eztituzte euscaldun guztiec legueac eta azturac bat, eta ez euscarazco minçatcea ere, ceren erresumac baitit.uzte different.
4 Ceren erresumac different baitituzte, ezta beraz cer miretsi, escualdunen artean içan dadin cembait differentcia mintçatceco maneretan; ceren herri batçuetacoec guehiago hantatcen eta gombertsatcen baitute erresuma batequin, bertce batçuec bertcearequin, eta hantacino hartaric bat-bederari lotcen çayo hitzcuntça arrotçaren cutsua, ceina ohi baita gambiaduraren orhantça eta levamia, non handic heldu baita emequi-emequi hitzcuntça gambiatcera, eta azquenean ossoqui iraunguitcera.
5 Badaquit Euscal-herrian anhitz moldez minçatcen direla, eta nori bere herrico euscara çaicala hoberenic eta ederrenic. Handic gogoac emaiten deraut ene esquiribatceco molde haur etçaiela guztiei ongui idurituco. Baiña nahi dut iaquin deçaten halacoec nic hitzcunça hunetan daquidana Saran ikhasia dudala, eta hango euscara ongui erabiltcen badut ez naicela gaitz erraiteco, eta ez arbuiatceco, ceren ezpaitaquit nic hangoa baicen. Ordea, ea Saraco euscara denz Euscal-Herrico hoberena eta garbiena, ez naiz ni hartara sartcen, bat-bederac emanen du bere iduriric. Eta Saraco euscara hunetçaz content eztenac esquiriba beça bertce euscara hobeago batez eta hobequiago, ez naiz ni hargatic bekhaiztuco, eta ez imbidios içanen.
6 Zuen eta gure iscuntza, escaras, aguitz differenta baita, pena dugu chit ezin explicatus zuen letra. Halla desiratzen guinduque zuec guri espaignoles escribatzea, eta guc zuei franseses edo escaras.

7 Baiña ceren comunzqui hala esquiribatcea nola minçatcea, nori berea iduritcen baitçaica hoberenic eta ederrenic, eta ene haur ez paita çurea beçala, ez othoi hargatic arbuya eta ez gaitz erran. Hunetçaz content ez pazara, eguiçu çuc ceure moldera, eta çure herrian usatcen eta seguitcen den beçala, ceren ez naiz ni hargatic beccaiztuco, eta ez mutturturic gaitzez iarrico.

8 Sucede a muchos bascongados que sólo tienen por buenos y elegantes los dialectos de su provincia, y es enfermedad común de los que hablan cualquier lenguaje (…). Pero es enfermedad de la pasión, que debe curarse con dos onzas de razón y de inteligencia.

9 El dialecto de Zuberoa, que, en lo hablado especialmente, es muy varonil y fuerte; y si por esto los labortanos le tachan de áspero, ellos se desquitan calificando al labortano de afeminado y melindroso, y siempre unos dialectos están murmurando de los otros con poca discreción.

10 En hacer comunes todas las voces hallo una dificultad casi invencible, y todo bascongado me la confesará desde luego. Y es la oposición con que los de un dialecto nacen y se crían contra los de dialecto diferente, especialmente en orden al lenguaje, en que mutuamente se tachan y desprecian por insensatas, y sin razón alguna. (…) Aunque uno y otro sepan v. gr. ambas voces, *dongea, gaistoa,* que significan "malo", el bizcaino jamás quiere usar del *gaistoa,* ni el guipuzcoano del *dongea.*

11 Como yo también oí a menudo en el país, los dialectos de los lugares más alejados son más semejantes en el uso de algunas palabras (…), que no los más próximos, que se repelen recíprocamente por celos de vecindad.

12 En bascuence no es posible escribir a gusto de todos. No sólo cada dialecto, sino hasta cada merindad, tiene sus modismos y términos favoritos, que prefieren a otros, aunque conozcan que son mejores los que usan otros.

13 Mi primera idea fue que toda esta Opera fuese en vascuence, pero luego me saltó la dificultad del dialecto de que me había de servir en ella. Si me valía del de Azkoitia hubiera sido poco grato a todo el resto del país hasta la frontera de Francia, por la preocupación que tienen contra el vascuence o dialecto de Goierri, y si quería usar del dialecto de Tolosa, Hernani, San Sebastián, etc. exponía a los actores a hacerse ridículos, pues sería difícil que todos pudiesen imitarle bien. Por esta razón, pues, me hube de contentar con reservar el vascuence para lo cantado, haciendo que todo lo representado fuese en castellano.

14 La primera objeción era decirnos que el bascuence es una lengua bárbara, incapaz de cultura, irreducible a método y Arte, y que era lengua áspera y desabrida.
   Los bascongados no parece que han hecho aprecio de ella, o a lo menos no le han explicado. Salen de su país, y hacen estudio de olvidarla, ni escriben, ni quieren siquiera escribir en su lengua una carta.

15 Y esto se confirma por las singularísimas ventajas del bascuence, y las perfecciones de su estructura, en que sino vence a todas, no parece que cede a ninguna: pues de cierto no puede ningún hombre ser autor de tan admirable harmonía.

16 Estrabón habla de las lenguas proprias y maternas de España, y que los españoles no usaban de una sola lengua vernácula y propria, sino de muchas, pero que esto era verdad de muchos dialectos de una misma lengua española, común a todas sus provincias, y que a estos dialectos llamó Estrabón lenguas distintas, y en fin, que aquella lengua española con sus diferentes dialectos era el bascuence.
   Esta lengua materna fue el bascuence, que es una lengua matriz, y que aun hoy tiene tantos dialectos y tan diversos, y por otra parte tan arreglados, y con raíces tan fijas, que con razón pueden llamarse *lengua bizcaina, lengua guipuzcoana, lengua alabesa, lengua navarra, lengua labortana,* y con todo eso no son más que dialectos de una misma lengua matriz que llamamos bascuence. Dialectos tan diferentes que apenas se entienden el guipuzcoano y bizcaino entre sí, ni el labortano y alabés, sino es habiendo particular estudio y reflexión.

17 El bascuence tiene su cuerpo de lengua, común y universal a todos sus dialectos. Este cuerpo del bascuence incluye todos los nombres y verbos tomados en sí mismos, esto es,

tomados como declinables y conjugables, y todas las demás partes de la oración, todos los modos del infinitivo, etc. en que no hay diferencia alguna. Los dialectos, pues, se reducen a las declinaciones del nombre y pronombre, que consisten en los artículos, y a las conjugaciones del verbo, que consisten en terminaciones o inflexiones diferentes.

18 Euskararen batasuna eratzekotz, gehien irasten den hizkalkia on harrtu beharr dugu, ez gehien mintzatzen datekena, literatura hizkuntza batuak, lehenez irakhurrtzekotz baitira. Zio honengatik gure literaturaren tradizino-hizkuntza harrtu beharr da, ta haur Leizarraga ganik, Atsular ganik, Etxeberri ganik, Haraneder ganik guganano ethorri den literatur-laburdara da.

19 Batzuek kultur-terminen orthographia euskaraldu (euren aburuz errazago bai-ta) beharr dela diote, euskararen phonetikari dagozkion legeak ezarrten derauztegularik. Sinhiste haur gezurrezkoa da. Kultur hitzek edozein hizkuntzatan eta kulturdun guztientzat heuren physiognomoni berezina dadukate, ta guk euskaraz kanpoko aspektu hori zaindu beharr dugu, liren errdaraz ikasten ditugun hitzak bezalakoak. Kultura ezta jente arruntena, bermailak kulturaren arazoetan ekhintzen eztu.

20 Bizkaitarrekin enaiz beiñ ere entenditu, beiñ ere. Berek yaten tzuten yolasa. *Tipttapttu* ... nola Frantzien xuberotarrek. Ni soldado egon nitzelaik banituen lagunek bizkaitarrak, konpañian. Ta ie enioten entenditzen eta azkenian aiek ere ez neri, pues asten ginen erderaz.

21 Frantzia mugakua o Naparruan ua zan da (…) erdeaz bate etzakiyan, batez, ta euskeaz ezin, ezin enteñidu alkarrekin. (…) Ta beste bat... au Bermeoko auetan e euskeia zailla, itxixa. Ta zeakua, bizkaittarrak e mordua euskaldunak, ta bat (…) gure euskeria ezin entenidu izate zuan. Or Bermeotik aurrera erri txiki batekua. (…) Guk entenitzen gendun dezente aena, baña beak ezin enteniu, ta erderaz itxe zuan askotan soldautzan. Erderaz baño obeto zakiyan are[k] euskeraz jakitez, baña etzan enteatze.

22 Géro, euskáras sálla da e. Guk, gu itzásuan ibílli geénak, bákisu betíro Biskáyan askótan, géyenatan Bermíon ta óitan ta, erdáras itz in biar e, erdáras eín biar alkárri.

23 It has been said that the devil himself abandoned his attempts to subvert the Basque Country because he was unable to learn its language. After living there for seven years, he had learned only two words, *bai* (yes) and *ez* (no). I don't know the origin of this myth, but it seems to have made notable headway at the time of the French Revolution of 1789. The French National Assembly decided to unite the Basque Country and Béarn in a single *département*. In an attempt to reverse this decision, the Basques brought up, among many things, the issue of linguistic diversity and, of course, the difficulty of Basque. If the devil had failed to learn Basque, how much more so the Béarnese? At the time, the argument made some sense. Today, when the goal is for all members of Basque society to be able to communicate with one another in Basque, it is inappropriate and negative.

References

Axular (Pedro Agerre). 1643. *Guero*. Bordeaux: G. Milanges.

Euskaltzaindia (Real Academia de la Lengua Vasca). 1999. *Euskal Herriko Hizkuntz Atlasa. Ohiko euskal mintzamoldeen antologia*. Bilbao.

Humboldt, Wilhelm F. von. 1958. *Primitivos pobladores de España y lengua vasca*. Translated by Francisco Echebarria. Madrid: Minotauro.

Krutwig, Federico. 1951. "Euskara Euskalerriaren Kultur-Bidea ledin izan". *Gernika*, nº 14, 8–11. Donibane Lohizune.

Krutwig, Federico. 1952. "Seminario yaunari ongi-etorria". *Euzko-Gogoa*, 3, nº 7–8, 29–30. Guatemala.

Krutwig, Federico. 1962. "Euskararen ethorkizuna". *Egan*, 20, nº 1–3, 19–33. Donostia: Diputación Foral de Gipuzkoa.

Larramendi, Manuel. 1729. *El impossible vencido. Arte de la Lengua Bascongada*. Salamanca: Antonio Joseph Villagordo Alcaráz.

Larramendi, Manuel. 1745. *Diccionario trilingüe del castellano, bascuence y latín*. Donostia: Bartolomé Riesgo y Montero.

Larramendi, Manuel. 1969. *Corografía o descripción general de la muy noble y muy leal provincia de Guipúzcoa*. (J. I. Tellechea Idigoras, ed.) Donostia: Sociedad Guipuzcoana de Ediciones y Publicaciones.

Leizarraga, Joanes. 1571. *Jesus Christ gure Jaunaren Testamendu Berria*. La Rochelle: Pierre Hautin. Facsímil: Donostia, Hordago, 1979.

Materra, Esteve. 1617. *Dotrina christiana*. (D. Krajewska, E. Zuloaga, E. Santazilia, B. Ariztimuño, O. Uribe-Etxebarria and U. Reguero, eds.) *Esteve Materraren Do(c)trina Christiana (1617 & 1623). Edizioa eta azterketa*. Bilbao: Real Academia de la Lengua Vasca and Universidad del País Vasco, 2017.

Mitxelena, Koldo. 1972. "Azken ordukoak". (P. Altuna, ed.) *Mitxelenaren idazlan hautatuak*: 365–401. Bilbao: Mensajero.

Moreno Cabrera, Juan Carlos. 2000. *La dignidad e igualdad de las lenguas. Crítica de la discriminación lingüística*. Madrid: Alianza.

Moreno Cabrera, Juan Carlos. 2007–2008. "Sobre la complejidad y dificultad de las lenguas. El caso del euskera". *Revista de Lenguas y Literaturas catalana, gallega y vasca*, 13: 199–216. Madrid: UNED.

Mujika, Serapio. 1908. "El vascuence en los archivos municipales de Guipúzcoa". Reprinted in *Revista Internacional de Estudios Vascos*, 2: 725–733. Bilbao: La Gran Enciclopedia Vasca, 1969.

Munibe, Xabier. 1762. *Gavon-Sariac*. Reprinted in (X. Altzibar, ed.) Gasteiz: Parlamento Vasco, 1991.

Munibe, Xabier. 1764. *El borracho burlado*. Reprinted in (X. Altzibar, ed.) Gasteiz: Parlamento Vasco, 1991.

Ruiz de Larrinaga, Juan (ed.). 1954–1958. "Cartas del P. Uriarte al Príncipe Luis Luciano Bonaparte". *Boletín de la Real Sociedad Vascongada de los Amigos del País*, 10: 231–302, 13: 220–239, 330–348, 429–452 and 14: 397–443. Donostia: Diputación Foral de Gipuzkoa.

Sagarzazu, Txomin. 2005. *Hondarribiko eta Irungo euskara*. Irun: Alberdania.

Tovar, Antonio. 1980. *Mitología e ideología sobre la lengua vasca*. Madrid: Alianza.

Txurruka, Alazne and Josune Urbieta. 2003. *Debako euskara*. Deba: Debako Ostolaza Kultur Elkartea.

Urkijo, Julio. 1907. *Obras vascongadas del doctor labortano Joannes d'Etcheberri (1712)*. Reprinted in *Revista Internacional de Estudios Vascos*, 28: 7–405. Bilbao: La Gran Enciclopedia Vasca, 1976.

Urkijo, Julio. 1919. *Los refranes de Garibay*. Reprinted in *Revista Internacional de Estudios Vascos*, 27: 493–694. Bilbao: La Gran Enciclopedia Vasca, 1976.

Villasante, Luis. 1952. "Literatur-euskara laphurrtarr klassikoaren gain eratua". *Boletín de la Real Sociedad Vascongada de los Amigos del País*, 8: 91–119 and 259–298. Donostia: Diputación Foral de Gipuzkoa.

5 Literary dialects

It is often said that the plan to standardise Basque was launched in 1964, but that is not entirely accurate. Several models were developed before 1964. However, they did not cover the whole of the Basque language community.

The first sketch of a standard language was elaborated by writers on the Lapurdian coast in the seventeenth century and was based on the speech of the region. These writers formed a very active and compact group, wrote works of quality, and followed similar guidelines. However, their movement was ephemeral. It can be said to have peaked between 1617, the year of publication of the first edition of Esteve Materra's doctrine (Materra 1617), and 1643, the year of publication of Pedro Agerre Axular's *Guero* (Axular 1643). After the first half of the seventeenth century, no more works worthy of mention seem to have been written within this school (Oyharçabal 2001).

Moreover, no writers outside the coastal region availed themselves of this language model, although it was known by others and taken into account. Zuberoan writers, for example, always used their own dialect. Another factor in the decline of the Lapurdian literary dialect was the loss of economic vitality along the coast after the late sixteenth century, first in the seventeenth century and then, even more definitively, in the second half of the eighteenth century.

The influence of Larramendi

In Larramendi's view, as we have seen, all dialects were harmoniously formed and organised and represented an extraordinary source of wealth for the language. On the basis of these principles, it is logical that he would favour cultivating all dialects, without giving priority to any. In passing, he intended to put an end to the dialect rivalries that so worried him. In short, his message was that there were no better or worse dialects, for all dialects were perfect and worth conserving.

To justify and defend his point of view, he sought support in ancient Greece, where each dialect specialised in a particular literary genre. This was clear from his grammar (Larramendi 1729: 13). Given his belief that in ancient Greece educated Greeks knew four dialects and Greeks who knew only one dialect were "idiots," he wanted a similar approach in the Basque Country:

> Since the true "Greek" was he who was able to use the different Greek dialects according to the literary genre of each, and not he who knew only that of his own region, the true "Basque" will be not he who knows only the Gipuzkoan dialect, or the Bizkaian, or the Navarrese, or the Lapurdian, but he who knows how to use all the dialects.[1]

In the prologue to the dictionary he returned to this idea (Larramendi 1745: CLX):

> The Greek authors used Greek in all their dialects, as they saw fit. [...] This freedom to speak and write in all dialects is what I would like to introduce to all Basques, so that a Gipuzkoan would speak Basque and write it in his dialect, which would always be the dominant one, but he would also use the other dialects when the opportunity arose. The same goes for Bizkaian, [...] Navarrese, Araban, and Lapurdian.[2]

Agustín Kardaberatz (1703–1770), another Jesuit and a personal friend of Larramendi, shared his view. I cite three fragments of his work *Eusqueraren berri onac* ("Good news about Basque"; Kardaberatz 1761), which was very influential at the time:

> Everyone must follow his own speech or dialect; that has been the habit and custom, and it will continue to be so in future (p. 13).
>
> They must get used [from childhood] to reading fluently and with ease not just the books written in their own dialect but those written in any of them, whether from France or from Navarre or Bizkaia (p. 19).
>
> It is absolutely essential and necessary to write in the three dialects of Bizkaia, Navarre, and Gipuzkoa (p. 63).[3]

Kardaberatz put his theory into practice and wrote two works in the Bizkaian dialect: *Dotrina cristiana edo cristiñau dotrinea* ("Christian doctrine") and *Jesus, Maria, ta Joseren devociñoco Libruchoric atararico devociño batzuc* ("Some prayers from the book of prayers devoted to Jesus, Mary, and Joseph"; Kardaberatz 1764).

Thanks to the esteem in which Larramendi and Kardaberatz were held, the dialect of the Gipuzkoan region of Beterri (the Donostia-Tolosa region) became a model of standard language starting in the second half of the eighteenth century and achieved notable success in a short period of time. As for the Bizkaian churchmen, they did not begin to write in their own dialect until the start of the nineteenth century.

In the mid-nineteenth century, Prince Bonaparte's intervention proved to be decisive, and he had numerous translations done in what he called the "literary dialects," that is, Lapurdian, Zuberoan, Gipuzkoan, and Bizkaian (Bonaparte 1863). Since his prime objective was to classify the Basque dialects, he endeavoured to mark their boundaries clearly and precisely, so that on many occasions he deliberately exaggerated the differences. He transmitted this idea to his close collaborators, for example José Antonio Uriarte. Uriarte, who had been charged by Bonaparte with translating the Bible into the Gipuzkoan dialect, perfectly assimilated his teachings. Thus, he let his master know (Ruiz de Larrinaga 1954: 251) that

> I use all the Basque authors, [...] taking from each what I deem best for doing the translation [...] of the Gipuzkoan dialect of Beterri; but, as far as possible, different from Bizkaian and Lapurdian, so that the difference between the dialects becomes apparent.[4]

To complete this panorama of the literary dialects, in the twentieth century a new one formed, Navarrese-Lapurdian, a synthesis of the speech of Lapurdi and Lower Navarre. It made its debut in 1944, with the publication of the priest Pierre Lafitte's *Grammaire Basque (navarro-labourdin littéraire)* (Lafitte 1944).

In short, the following five language models were current in the Basque Country:

1   The dialect of the Lapurdian coast, during the first half of the seventeenth century.
2   Zuberoan, starting in the seventeenth century.
3   Gipuzkoan, starting in the eighteenth century.
4   Bizkaian, divided into two, after the nineteenth century.
5   Navarrese-Lapurdian, during the twentieth century.

These five literary dialects had, in one sense, a positive outcome: generally speaking, they promoted the unity of the language, each within its own area of operation. However, they hampered unity on a wider basis, that of the Basque language as a whole. What is worse, in seeking to delimit as clearly as possible the frontiers of each separate dialect, they exaggerated and deepened its special features, so that as a result dialect differences have widened and deepened. The main victim of this process has been the Bizkaian dialect.

The Bizkaian standard dialect

The start of this standard dialect, in the early nineteenth century, had two truly lamentable consequences. On the one hand, it distanced itself from the rest of the Basque dialects and, on the other, within the dialect itself, deepened the differences between its two (or, in Bonaparte's opinion, three) subdialects.

The subdialects of Bizkaian

The Gipuzkoan Jesuit Agustín Kardaberatz was the first to point to the existence of two varieties of Bizkaian. In his prologue to *Cristiñau dotrinea*,
written in the mid-eighteenth century but unpublished until the twentieth
century, he drew a line that went from north to south: from Cape Matxitxako,
between Bermeo and Bakio, as far as Otxandio, on the border with Araba
(Kardaberatz 1973). Despite the passage of time, I believe that this division
still holds today.

It is difficult, if not impossible, to determine the provenance of Bizkaian
texts from before the nineteenth century, particularly the shorter ones. From
the nineteenth century onwards, it becomes easier to guess the subdialect to
which they belonged, sound evidence that dialect differences were becoming
more salient.

On the other hand, the speech of the Gipuzkoan valley of Deba was drawing
away from Bizkaia and approximating more to Gipuzkoa. Most of the Bizkaian
innovations that I consider as postdating the nineteenth century have not penetrated this valley. This is the case, for example, of the root -*e*- in the verb "to
have," in forms such as *dekot* "I have" and *dekozu* "you have" (*daukat* and
daukazu in standard Basque) used in most of Bizkaia but not in the Deba Valley.

On the contrary, in the speech of the Deba Valley we already find some
innovations that are Gipuzkoan or common to all the dialects but have not
yet reached the province of Bizkaia, with the exception of some places bordering on Gipuzkoa, like Ermua, Elorrio, and Ondarroa. An example is the
morpheme -*te* in the second person plural of verbs of absolutive type* (*zarete*
"you are" and *zatozte* "you come"), habitual in the north of the Deba Valley,
as well as in a large part of the centre of the Basque Country, which in Bizkaia is -*(i)e* (*zarie, zatoze*).

Probably on this basis, Bonaparte considered the speech of the Deba Valley
to be the third subdialect of Bizkaian. In my opinion, it does not meet the
conditions for such a distinction, but I fully understand Bonaparte's procedure.

In any case, whether there are two or three subdialects, what is clear is that
this division was sharpened by the creation of standard Bizkaian.

The Mogel way

The priest Juan Antonio Mogel (1745–1804), who was the forerunner and
main leader of the Basque renaissance in Bizkaia, wrote his first work in
Gipuzkoan dialect, taking Agustín Kardaberatz as his guide. He explained
the reason for his decision (Mogel 1800: XIII–XIV):

> I am convinced that the Basque language of this book will be understood
> throughout Gipuzkoa, in many towns of Bizkaia, and in most of Navarre.
> Kardaberatz's books are easier to understand in all corners of the Basque
> Country, and I have endeavoured to imitate him for that reason.[5]

The decision unleashed a fierce controversy in Bizkaia and, apparently, the ecclesiastics of that province declared themselves absolutely against it. This was recognised by Mogel himself (Villasante 1964: 63):

> No sooner did news of the appearance of a work in Basque and in the Gipuzkoan dialect reach Bizkaia [...] and that its author was a priest of the same place than general uproar broke out among the Bizkaian churchmen, with bitter complaints that the Gipuzkoans had been given preference. What use to us, they said, is a work written in a strange and complicated dialect? The author could give powerful reasons for his conduct, or for his supposed predilection for the Gipuzkoan dialect if necessary.[6]

He made known his "powerful reasons" in 1803, when he published a version of the book in Bizkaian dialect (Mogel 1803: I–II):

> I come, finally, to offer you what has so insistently been asked of me, the book that I published in the Gipuzkoan dialect on the sacrament of confession. If I had seen among the Bizkaians the same interest in Basque that I observed among the Gipuzkoans, I would not have left my fellow countrymen in the dark. But I do not regret the decision I made. I have found to my immense satisfaction that almost a thousand copies of the book have been sold in Navarre, Gipuzkoa, and Bizkaia. I have learned that many priests read it in the churches and not a few farmers read it in their homes. I admit, and I must confess, that Bizkaians of the interior will find it difficult to understand the Gipuzkoan dialect without a great deal of effort, but the odd word that they do not know will be understandable alongside the others, in context.[7]

The rupture

Following the controversy unleashed around Mogel, a group of churchmen began taking the first steps towards the constitution of a Bizkaian standard dialect. Mogel followed a very different path. He wrote in Gipuzkoan dialect or in Castilian works destined for a wide and educated reading public. For example, when the linguist Wilhelm von Humboldt requested him to translate texts from Salustio, Tacitus, Livy, and Cicero into Basque, he did so in Gipuzkoan (Garate 1934 [1972]: 623). The rest of the works, including his famous *Dr Peru Abarca*, were in Bizkaian, but invariably in the speech of Markina, where he lived and developed his pastoral work. This too displeased the churchmen, and the rupture was complete.

In general, the writers of the eastern part of Bizkaia or, to put it another way, those of Durango and Lea-Artibai (the area of Lekeitio, Ondarroa, Markina, and their surroundings) followed Mogel. Those from the Bizkaia interior took another route, based on a type of language closer to their own.

The Gipuzkoans of the Deba Valley sided with neither, and since the priests who preached in their churches were generally from Gipuzkoa and not from Bizkaia, they were more exposed to the influence of that dialect.

In the mid-nineteenth century, Prince Bonaparte came out clearly for the Basque of Markina, that of Mogel. He always ordered that the translations into standard Bizkaian be made in this variety, even if it displeased José Antonio Uriarte, who was usually the one in charge of carrying out the translations.

In the late nineteenth and early twentieth centuries, the controversy reopened. Sabino Arana Goiri, founder of the Basque Nationalist Party, came out in favour of the Basque of Markina, which the lexicographer R. M. Azkue considered to be too local. Why did Arana Goiri, a Bilbaoan by birth and residence, opt for the Markina dialect? Probably due to the influence of the well-known Durango writer Pablo Pedro Astarloa (1752–1806). Whatever the case, after Sabino Arana Goiri, Markina Basque was scarcely ever used in literature.

Bizkaian in relation to the other Basque dialects

Even worse than the internal division of the Bizkaian dialect was its remoteness and isolation from the rest of the dialects. The distancing of the Bizkaian dialect from the rest and its internal fragmentation happened in the nineteenth century, as a result of the zeal with which some activists tried consolidate standard Bizkaian.

The vision of the dialects in Bizkaia in the early nineteenth century

In the early nineteenth century, in the opinion of those who began writing in Bizkaian, the differences between the dialects – Bizkaian included – were neither many nor great. Three writers whose work was highly relevant to this issue were Juan Antonio Mogel, Pedro Antonio Añibarro, and Bartolomé Madariaga. In Mogel's case, there is a clear desire to minimise the differences. Referring to the distance between Bizkaian and Gipuzkoan, which all scholars agree is where the dialect barrier is clearest and most abrupt, he went as far as to say (Villasante, 1964: 63–64):

> The auxiliary verbs in both dialects are, in short, the same. The syntax is the same, and the articular declension of the nouns is the same, except in the ablative of the Castilian preposition *con* ("with"), which is *quin* in Gipuzkoan and *gaz* and *caz* in Bizkaian, differences with which all Basques are familiar. Very many and by far the greater part of the words in both dialects have the same meaning. The variety that occurs in others is of a single letter, *eman/emon* ["give"], *dot/det* ["I have it"], *nas/naiz* ["I am"], *ipini/ifini/imini* ["put"], *idoró/ediró* ["discover"], and *arquitu/aurquitu* ["find"]. [...] In sum, the sole obstacle is that Bizkaians of the interior do not know the meaning of various [Gipuzkoan] words.[8]

The same desire to downplay dialect differences can be found in his essay *La historia y geografía de España ilustradas por el idioma vascuence* ("The history and geography of Spain as illustrated by the Basque language"), although this work did not see the light until a century later (Mogel 1935 [Garate, ed.]: 262):

> The Basque language has dialects that are less different than those of Castilian, Galician, and Portuguese, and the Basques, Navarrese, Gipuzkoans, and Bizkaians understand each other more easily than Galicians, Castilians, and Lusitanians.[9]

Bartolomé Madariaga (1768–1838), a Carmelite friar and one of the best Bizkaian writers of the time, also emphasised the unity of the language. It is interesting to look at the reasons (with which I fully concur) to which he attributes the origin of dialect differences (Madariaga 1828 [1988]: 500–501):

> I can say that Basque is unitary in terms of its grammatical syntax; and that the difference is in the mode of pronunciation, and in some provincial and even local terms, born of the fact that the language exists and is kept alive among inhabitants of many mountains with little or no relation to each other that might make their individual dialects more uniform. [...] Basque is one and the same in all the Basque provinces.[10]

Añibarro (1748–1830) also refused to see the differences as insurmountable. The verb and, of course, the vocabulary were the two biggest obstacles. In his grammar, written in the early nineteenth century but published in the second half of the twentieth (Añibarro 1969 [Villasante, ed.]: 14), he said:

> Once the conjugation has been mastered, it is no harder to learn the meaning of the words than in the case of other languages.[11]

The perception of the Bizkaian dialect in the twentieth century

In the early twentieth century, Manuel Arriandiaga (1876–1947), author of several grammatical studies, already noted some important differences within the Bizkaian dialect which – and this is important – had their origin according to him in the remote past (Arriandiaga 1907 [1969]: 670):

> If one looks closely at the Bizkaian people, it is clear that they are a distinct people within the Basque family. The most convincing reason lies in the Bizkaian dialect. We Basques all have one Basque language, for Basque is one and only one. But in Bizkaia this Basque is markedly different from that in other regions of Euzkadi [the Basque Country]. This marked dialect difference determines a difference of tribe within the Basque family or race.[12]

The opinion of Koldobika Eleizalde (1873–1923), author of several grammatical essays, and a person well known in his time (Eleizalde 1911: 268), was even more radical:

> Perhaps it would be more proper to speak of Euzkeric languages than of dialects. But in that case the tongues would no longer be three but two, since the Pyrenean dialect [spoken in Zuberoa and Lower Navarre] could be grouped together with the Vasconic [spoken in Lapurdi, Navarre, and Gipuzkoa], and two Basque languages would result: Bizkaian and non-Bizkaian; the latter might be called Basque. It seems to me that between the two there is the same degree of difference as between Spanish and Portuguese, for example.[13]

This opinion became mainstream. For example, in 1924 an important work, *Les langues du monde* ("Languages of the world"), was published under the direction of the well-known French linguists Antoine Meillet and Marcel Cohen. Georges Lacombe was charged with writing the section on the Basque language. In it he said (Lacombe 1924 [1952]: 260–261):

> We believe that it would be enough to distinguish two big dialect groups: Bizkaian (which could also be called Western Basque) on the one hand, and the rest of the dialects on the other. The latter group could be called, in opposition to the former, central-eastern. We base this classification on the following consideration: one passes through imperceptible gradations among the dialects that make up the latter group, while the jump is rather abrupt when we move from Gipuzkoan to Bizkaian. In fact, the latter differs in an important part of the conjugation, through the use of auxiliaries that are peculiar to it; presents typical peculiarities in many grammatical aspects, to a greater extent than the rest of the dialects; and, finally, contains within its lexicon a large number of words unknown in the other dialects.[14]

The Dutch linguist Christianus Cornelis Uhlenbeck (1866–1950) gave new impetus to this theory. According to him, it might be a case of dialects distinct in origin that later, with the passage of time, grew closer to each other. This manner of reasoning is habitually found among those seeking to demonstrate the special character of Bizkaian. If two forms coexist within this dialect, one common to all Basque dialects and the other exclusive to Bizkaian, they consider that the latter is indigenous to Bizkaia and the other imported from Gipuzkoa. Uhlenbeck (1947) argues as follows (544):

> If we look at the peculiarities that characterise Bizkaian, we get the impression that it is necessary to start from two ancient Western Pyrenean dialects, which at a certain point were not neighbours but, in the course of time, as a result of contact, began to approximate to one

another. From one of them Bizkaian would emerge and, from the other, the rest of the dialects spoken on Spanish and French territory. The drawing together of Bizkaian and Gipuzkoan or, to put it in another way, the gradual disappearance of the undoubtedly clear limits in ancient times, is a process that started a long time ago and still continues.[15]

Reasons for the change in viewpoints

What happened in the course of a century to cause people to view things so differently? Why did people stop talking about the unity between the dialects and start saying that Bizkaian was very different? The answer is simple. The authors of grammatical studies did their best to emphasise the distinct personality of the Bizkaian dialect. To that end, they stressed what they considered to be specific to that dialect, its spontaneously emerging innovations in certain places in Bizkaia in recent times. The Bilbaoan Franciscan friar Juan Mateo Zabala (1777–1840) played a prominent role in this matter. He published the first grammar of the Bizkaian dialect, in 1848, in which he defended some really surprising points of view (Zabala 1848: 56):

> I say nothing about Lekeitio's *ebazan* ["he had them"], *ebeezan* ["they had them"], *nebazan* ["I had them"], or Orozko's *ebazan* and *ebeezan*; nor about the *nendun* ["I had it"], *nenduzan* ["I had them"], *eudeezan* ["they had them"] of the entire centre of Bizkaia, which are undoubtedly more in keeping with the rest of the conjugation, than the *zituan* ["he had them"], *zituen* ["they had them"], and *nituan* ["I had them"] that our writers have adopted.[16]

Zabala believed that the verbal forms of the *zituan* type, which were used in all the Basque dialects and in most of Bizkaia, had been "imported" by Bizkaian writers. As for forms of the *ebazan* type, which were used only in two places in Bizkaia (Orozko and Lekeitio), they were, according to him, the indigenous and ancient forms.

Zabala's reasoning was based on the fact that forms of the *ebazan* type contained the pluralising element *-z*, characteristic of the Bizkaia dialect, so that these were supposed to be original to that dialect. What actually happened is that speakers of the two places had extended the *-z* to all types of verbal inflections. In other words, a few Bizkaian speakers had "regularised" the language, in the same way, for example, that English speakers sometimes, as children, use the "regular" form "knowed" instead of "knew," which is "irregular" but right.

He also considered as authentic and genuine forms of the *nendun* type, used in central Bizkaia. They were also modern forms, products of speakers' analogic and regularising action. In fact, given the forms *gendun* ("we had it"), *zendun* ("you had it"), and *zenduen* ("you [plural] had it"), in some towns there spontaneously arose the regular form *nendun* ("I had it"), instead of the usual – but irregular – *neban*.

Naturally, Zabala's reasoning was completely wrong, but in his grammar he took "regularity" as his main criterion, with the two consequences outlined above. On the one hand, Bizkaian became even more distant from the rest of the dialects, and on the other, this new Bizkaian also moved away from the language most of the inhabitants of Bizkaia habitually spoke.

Linguistic experiments in Bizkaia

Throughout the difficult and perilous history of Basque, there have naturally been many attempts to revive and revitalise it and, again naturally, some have been successful and others have gone wrong. I now go on to discuss two experiments that went wrong. Both were centred on Bilbao, and their consequences have been devastating. The main victim has, once again, been the Bizkaian dialect, which, as I have already shown, has since the early nineteenth century suffered all kinds of misfortunes. The experiments can be called (a) purism and (b) the reconstruction of original Basque.

Purism

In the late nineteenth century, purist tendencies were deeply rooted within the Basque language, as a result of the activities of Sabino Arana Goiri (1865–1903). He was acting out of political principle: according to him, the Basque Country had the right to claim sovereignty, since Basques were a completely different people from those in Spain and France. Arana Goiri considered that racially, culturally, and in terms of their customs and, of course, language, the Basques were different.

Basque, like every language in contact with other languages, has absorbed a huge number of loans through its contacts, and Arana Goiri saw his mission as eliminating them. That meant having to invent substitutes, an enormous task, but that did not intimidate the Bilbaoan political. He reformed the Basque book of saints (Arana Goiri 1897, 1898), and ever since then Basques have used totally new personal names, such as *Ander* (Andrew), *Andoni* (Anthony), *Gorka* (George), *Gotzon* (Angel), *Joseba* (Joseph), *Josu* (Jesus), *Julen* (Julian), *Kepa* (Peter), *Koldobika* (Louis), *Miren* (Mary), and *Sorkunde* (Conception), all of which have survived to this day. He also reformed the numbers system (Arana Goiri 1901a), eliminated all the words of Latin origin from the Basque version of the Lord's Prayer (Arana Goiri 1901b), proposed numerous fantastic etymologies, and invented a myriad of new words (see Pagola 2005).

Arana Goiri counted on a multitude of followers and, in a short period of time, wrought a complete metamorphosis of Basque. So much so that it became unrecognisable to Basques themselves, who called it *euzkera berri* (new Basque). Given the difficulty that attaches to learning such an exotic language, not even his own supporters used it in daily life, except in a few brief texts and speeches. Otherwise, and particularly in personal relations, they usually used Castilian. Justo Mokoroa (1901–1990), in a work published

in 1936, *Genio y lengua* ("Genius and language"), summarised the characteristics of Arana Goiri's new language. Here are some examples (Mokoroa
1936: 89):

a   In the name of the mythological fetish called "purism," hundreds of
    words in daily and time-honoured use have been anathematised and out-
    lawed, notwithstanding their prestige, poetic value, and evocative virtue;
    deflowering the living language, and depriving it of aroma and charm.
b   The neologism and "reform" mania has reached a level of excess that in
    other languages would seem monstrous, and there is no reason why it
    should not also be so in ours.
c   With all these things, there has emerged not a bookish and more or less
    indigestible style but a gibberish, a true argot, which already has a name,
    euskera berry [new Basque]; which could not fail to give the Basque
    people indigestion. And, in fact, its deadening insensitivity repels every-
    where as intrusive, violent, artificial, and unpleasant.[17]

In Mokoroa's opinion, the consequence of the reform was as follows
(Mokoroa 1936: 92):

The result of all these mistakes was foreseeable and is today lamentable: *a
reduction in the use of Basque.* [18]

Nevertheless, many of the terms invented by Arana Goiri continue to
enjoy great vitality in contemporary Basque. They include the following:
aberri (fatherland), *abertzale* (patriot), *abesti* (song), *abeslari* (singer),
abestu (sing), *abizen* (surname), *aintza* (glory), *a(ha)lguztidun* (all-mighty),
antzeztu (represent), *antzoki* (theatre), *(h)arpidedun* (subscriber), *aurkezpen*
(presentation), *batzoki* (meeting place), *bazkide* (partner, affiliate), *berbiz-
kunde* (resurrection), *biltoki* (warehouse), *egutegi* (calendar), *ereserki*
(hymn), *espetxe* (prison), *Euzkadi* (Basque Country), *garagardo* (beer),
gipuzkera (Gipuzcoan dialect), *goiburu* (slogan), *gorpuzkinak* (mortal
remains), *idatzi* (write), *ikastola* (school), *ikur* (sign), *ikurrin* (flag), *iragarle*
(prophet), *(h)izki* (letter), *onespen* (blessing), *ordezkari* (representative),
pizkunde (renaissance), *sendi* (family), *ugaztun* (mammal), *urtaro* (season of
the year), and *zenbaki* (number).

The reconstruction of original Basque

This trend also emerged in the late nineteenth century and was even more
radical than the purist trend. Its adherents thought that given the adverse
conditions that Basque had endured, it was in a state of total decomposition
and decline, so the best solution would be to return it to its original state.
Naturally, nobody knew what Basque looked like at the time of its formation,
so the only option was to reinvent it.

The pioneer of this trend was the Bizkaian priest Resurrección María Azkue (1864–1951), who later became the life president of the Academy of the Basque Language. In 1891 he published a grammar, *Euskal-Izkindea* (Azkue 1891), in which he demonstrated his architectual skills (see Laka 1986–1987).

Here is an example of Azkue's procedure. For the first person of the verb "to be," the various dialects of Basque use the following inflection: *naiz/niz/ naz*. All were corrupt in Azkue's view, for the final *-z* was, according to him, a plural morpheme, while the first person is obviously singular. So, the original form must have been *nai*.

The third person singular of the verb "to be" is *da*, in all dialects, but for Azkue this was a contraction, since *-ai-* should figure in the root, so the primitive verbal form would have been *dai*.

The third person plural of the verb "to be" is *dira* in all dialects. Here, two changes were required. On the one hand, it was necessary to restore the complete form *-ai-* in the root and, on the other, to add the plural morpheme *-z*. So, the pure form would be *daiz*.

The following list represents the conjugation of the verb *izan* (to be) in Basque. The middle column shows the current standard Basque forms, while the right-hand column shows Azkue's proposals.

/standard Basque/ /Azkue/
I am /*naiz* /*nai*
You are /*haiz*/*ai*
It/he/she is /*da*/*dai*
We are /*gara*/*gaiz*
You are (plural) /*zarete*/*zaiz*
They are /*dira*/*daiz*

The consequences of this experiment were very negative, and among its chief victims were, undoubtedly, the students of the Bilbao Institute, where Azkue occupied the chair of Basque. Apparently, the number of students who took the exams was minimal, which worried even the Provincial Government in Bizkaia. A member of the commission that looked into the case said (Laka 1986–1987: 417):

> Since we are talking about this subject, I must say that one year I attended these exams and did not understand a word of the Basque taught by the professor; and I would therefore propose that this teaching be dropped or given in another form.[19]

The road opened by Azkue, which he later dismissed as a "youthful sin," had numerous followers, prominent among them the Bizkaian cleric Manuel Arriandiaga (see Laka 1986–1987: 727–811). Much later, in 1922, the Bizkaian Capuchin monk Saturnino Soloeta (1881–1964) published a long essay in Buenos Aires (Soloeta 1922), where he revealed the structure that, in his opinion, Basque had had at the time of its formation. By mid-century, even the well-known writer Nikolas Ormaetxea *Orixe* (1888–1961) wrote articles supporting Azkue's approach (see, especially, Ormaetxea 1950, 1959, 1961).

Some reflections on the future

Ever since the early nineteenth century, Basque has run a chequered course in Bizkaia. On the one hand, deliberate attempts have been made to distance Bizkaian from the other dialects, while on the other hand it has been abused and disfigured: features were revived that had been forgotten, many localisms were revitalised, and the dialect fell foul of all sorts of purist currents and chimerical experiments. All that has necessitated restorative work that must, in my opinion, contain at least the following threads:

a   The Bizkaians must regain confidence in their dialect. They must assume that this dialect is not better than the others, but also that it is no less good than, say, Gipuzkoan or Lapurdian

b   The Bizkaians must understand that their dialect is just one among several Basque dialects. It is a very particular dialect, but nevertheless just one among several. This means, among other things, that the standard norm for Basque also applies in Bizkaia and that Bizkaians must know and use it. On the other hand, Bizkaians too can and must make a contribution to that standard, since it is their property. It is therefore inappropriate for some groups in Bizkaia to want to promote a standard Bizkaian. At best, this is a recipe from the past that has, as we have seen, led only to disaster. At the present time, when a standard norm is available to all Basques, it is logical to apply it to Bizkaia too, although with all adaptations deemed appropriate, especially in the lexicon.

c   A detailed study of the Bizkaian dialect is needed to determine what is ancient and what is modern, what is characteristic and what is invented, what is general and what is local. Such studies have, in part, already been made, but they need to be reworked, updated, and divulged to a wider audience (see, among others, Lafon 1944, Tovar 1959: 146–177, Mitxelena 1964 [1988]: 13–22, Mitxelena 1981, Lakarra 1997: 147–198, and Zuazo 2017). These tasks are urgent and vital, given that almost half of all Basques, more than 1,100,000 people, live in Bizkaia.

Notes

1   Pues como no sólo se llamaba "griego" el que hablaba algún dialecto particular suyo, sino mucho más el que no estando atado a ninguno, usaba de todos los dialectos en la ocasión: así también se ha de llamar "vascongado", no sólo el que habla el dialecto guipuzcoano, o el bizcaíno, o el navarro, y labortano, sino también y con más razón el que hace familiares suyos a todos los dialectos.

2 Los autores griegos usaban de su lengua griega en todos sus dialectos, según les parecía convenir (…). Esta libertad de hablar y escribir en todos los dialectos es la que yo quisiera introducir en todos los bascongados, de manera que el guipuzcoano hablase el bascuence y le escribiese en su dialecto, que fuese siempre el dominante, pero se valiese también de los demás dialectos según la oportunidad de las circunstancias. Lo mismo digo del bizcaino (…), lo mismo es del navarro, alabés y labortano.

3 Bacoitzac bere dialecto edo izquerari jarraitu ondo: oitura, usu ta costumbrea ala da, ta aurrera ere ala izango da. […] Oitu bear dira, ez emengo izqueran bacarric, ezpada edoceñ dialectotan, eta Francia, edo Nafarroaco, edo Bizcaico libruetan ondo ta trebe iracurtera. […] Bizcaico, Nafarroaco, ta Gipuzcoaco iru dialectoetan escribitcea guztiz premiazco ta gauza chit bearra da.

4 Hago uso de todos los autores bascongados (…) tomando de cada uno lo que creo mejor para hacer la traducción (…) del dialecto guipuzcoano de Beterri; pero, en cuanto se pueda, diferente del vizcaíno y labortano, a fin de que se conozca la diferencia de los dialectos.

5 Uste det berriz libru onetaco eusquera izango dala aditua Guiputz gucian, Vizcaico erri ascotan, ta Naparroa gueienean. Cardaverasen libruac aditzen errazagoac dira Euscal-errietan (…). Nic ere oni jarraitu diot aleguinez arrazoi beragatic.

6 Apenas se tuvo noticia en Vizcaya, que salía a luz una obra bascongada y en dialecto guipuzcoano (…), y que su autor era un cura de dicho señorío, cuando se suscitó una conmoción como general entre los eclesiásticos vizcaynos, con quexas amargas de haber sido preferidos los guipuzcoanos. ¿Qué utilidad podemos sacar, se decían, de una obra escrita en un dialecto extraño e intrincado para nosotros? El autor podría dar razones poderosas de su proceder, o de la atribuida predilección, si fuera del caso el publicarlas.

7 Orra nos aguertuten nachatzun aspaldi onetan escatuten cendubana emotera, ta zan quiputz eusqueran arguitu dodan Confesinuaren gañeco liburuba. Nic icusi baneu bizcaitarretan eusqueriaren zaletasun quiputzetan necusana, ez nintzan ain esquer dongacua izango, cein da ichico nituban baruric neure bizcaitarrac. […] Ez dot damu artu neban asmo ta nequia. Neure biotzeco pocic andijenagaz icusi dot, celan zabaldu dirian milla bat liburu Naparroa, Gipuzkoa, ta Bizcaijan. Jaquin dot abade jaun ascoc iracurten ditubezala elessetan, ta nequezale ez guichic euren echeetan. […] Bazaut, autor dot, ta ez daucat aztuta bizcaitar barrucuentzat gach izango dala quiputz eusqueria ondo aditutia. Baña verba ascatu adituten ez dirianac, aditu oy dira lotu ta catetuta dagozan beztiacaz batera.

8 Los verbos auxiliares de ambos dialectos son en suma los mismos, la misma la sintaxis, una misma la declinación articular de los nombres, excepto en el ablativo de la preposición castellana *con,* que se diferencian por *quin* guipuzcoano, *gaz* y *caz* vizcaynos, cuya diferencia la saben todos los bascongados. Muchísimos y la mucha mayor parte de los vocablos de ambos dialectos tienen la misma significación. La variedad que se nota en otros, es de sola una u otra letra, *eman/emon, dot/det, nas/naiz, ipini/ifini/imini, idoró/ediró, arquitu/aurquitu* (…). En suma el único embarazo está en que los vizcaynos de lo interior ignoran el significado de varios vocablos.

9 El idioma vascongado tiene unos dialectos de menos diferencia que los dialectos castellano, gallego y portugués y se entenderían más fácilmente los vascongados, navarros, guipuzcoanos y vizcaínos que los gallegos, castellanos y lusitanos.

10 Puedo decir que el bascuence es uno en su sintaxis gramatical; y la diferencia es en el modo de la pronunciación, y algunos términos provinciales, y aun locales, nacido de que esta lengua existe, y se conserva de viva voz entre habitantes de muchas montañas con poca, o ninguna relación entre sí, para el efecto de uniformar su singular dialecto. (…) El bascuence es uno en todas las provincias bascongadas.

11 Vencida la conjugación, no cuesta más que en otras lenguas el aprender los significados de las voces.

12 Examinando con atención al pueblo vizcaíno, vemos claramente ser un pueblo distinto dentro de la familia vasca. La razón más convincente está en el dialecto vizcaíno. Los vascos poseemos todos un euzkera, pues el euzkera no es más que uno. Pero ese euzkera tiene en Bizkaya diferencias muy señaladas de las que en otras regiones de Euzkadi. Esta diferencia dialectal tan marcada determina diferencia de tribu dentro de la familia o raza vasca.

13 Quizá sería más propio hablar de lenguas euzkéricas que de dialectos. Pero entonces las lenguas no serían ya tres, sino dos, puesto que el dialecto pirenaico podría agruparse con el vascón, y resultarían dos lenguas vascas: la bizkaina y la no-bizkaina; a esta última podría denominársela vascona. Yo creo que entre ambas hay tanta diferencia como entre el español y el portugués, por ejemplo.

14 Il nous semble qu'il serait suffisant de distinguer deux grands groupes dialectaux: le biscayen (que l'on pourrait appeler aussi basque occidental) d'un côté, et de l'autre côté tous les autres dialectes. [...] On pourrait appeler ce groupe, par opposition au premier, centro-oriental. Nous justifierions ce classement par la considération suivante: on passe par gradations insensibles d'un dialecte à l'autre parmi ceux qui constituent ce groupe, tandis que le saut est assez brusque quand on passe du guipuskoan au biscayen. Ce dernier se distingue en effet, dans toute une partie de sa conjugaison, par l'emploi d'auxiliaires qui lui sont propres, il offre des particularités typiques dans maints détails de la grammaire en plus grand nombre que les autres dialectes, et enfin son vocabulaire a souvent des mots non compris des autres Basques.

15 Si nous faisons attention aux particularités individualisantes du biscayen par rapport aux autres dialectes basques, nous avons plutôt l'impression qu'il nous faut partir de deux dialectes pyrénéens occidentaux anciens qui, pendant une certaine période, n'étaient pas immédiatement voisins, mais qui, entrés plus tard en contact immédiat, se sont rapprochés de plus en plus. De l'un serait donc issu le biscayen; du second, tous les autres dialectes en territoires espagnol et français. Le rapprochement entre le biscayen et le guipuskoan, en d'autres mots l'effacement graduel des limites indubitablement nettes autrefois, est un procès en cours longtemps et qui se poursuit toujours.

16 Nada digo del *ebazan, ebeezan, nebazan* de Lequeitio, y aun los dos primeros de Orozco; ni del *nendun, nenduzan, eudeezan* de todo el centro de Vizcaya, que sin duda son de una formación más conforme al resto de la conjugación, que *zituan, zituen, nituan* que han adoptado nuestros escritores.

17 *a)* En nombre del fetiche mitológico llamado "purismo" se han anatemizado y proscrito centenares de voces de uso diario e inmemorial, no obstante su prestancia, valor poético y virtud evocadora; desflorando el lenguaje vivo, y privándolo de aroma y encanto.

b) La manía del neologismo y de la "reforma" ha llegado a excesos que en otras lenguas parecerían monstruosos y no hay razón para que no lo sean en la nuestra.

c) Con todas estas cosas se ha forjado, no ya un estilo libresco más o menos indigesto, sino una jerigonza, un verdadero *argot,* que ya tiene su nombre conocido, *euskera berri;* el cual no podía menos de empachársele al pueblo euskaldun, y, en efecto, la sensibilidad aún no embotada de éste rechaza en todas partes por intruso, violento, artificial y antipático.

18 Resultado de todos estos extravíos ha sido el que era de prever y hoy lamentamos: *reducción del uso del euskera.*

19 Ya que se habla de ese asunto, he de manifestar que yo concurrí un año a esos exámenes y no entendí una palabra del vascuence que en esa cátedra se enseña; y por ello propondría que se suprimiera esa enseñanza o se diera en otra forma.

References

Añibarro, Pedro Antonio. 1969. *Gramática bascongada*. (L. Villasante, ed.) *Anuario del Seminario de Filología Vasca "Julio de Urquijo"*, 3: 3–169. Donostia: Diputación Foral de Gipuzkoa.

Arana Goiri, Sabino. 1897. *Egutegi bizkattarra*. Reprinted in *Obras Completas de Sabino Arana Goiri* (ii): 983–1115. Donostia: Sendoa, 1980.

Arana Goiri, Sabino. 1898. *Lenengo egutegi bizkattarra*. Reprinted in *Obras Completas de Sabino Arana Goiri* (ii): 1401–1659. Donostia: Sendoa, 1980.

Arana Goiri, Sabino. 1901a. *Análisis y reforma de la numeración euzkérica*. Reprinted in *Obras Completas de Sabino Arana Goiri* (iii): 1829–1880 . Donostia: Sendoa, 1980.

Arana Goiri, Sabino. 1901b. *Análisis y corrección del Pater Noster del euzkera usual*. Reprinted in *Obras Completas de Sabino Arana Goiri* (iii): 1881–1969. Donostia: Sendoa, 1980.

Arriandiaga, Manuel. 1907. "Euzkera ala Euskera?". *Revista Internacional de Estudios Vascos*, 1: 642–672. Reprinted in Bilbao: La Gran Enciclopedia Vasca, 1969.

Axular (Pedro Agerre). 1643. *Guero*. Bordeaux: G. Milanges.

Azkue, Resurrección M. 1891. *Euskal-Izkindea/Gramática eúskara*. Bilbao: Astuy.

Bonaparte, Louis-Lucien. 1863. *Carte des sept provinces basques, montrant la délimitation actuelle de l'euscara*. London.

Eleizalde, Koldobika. 1911. "Raza, lengua y nación vascas". *Euzkadi*, 8, nº 10, 268–276. Bilbao.

Garate, Justo. 1934. "Cinco cartas inéditas de Guillermo de Humboldt". *Revista Internacional de Estudios Vascos*, 25: 622–639. Reprinted in Bilbao: La Gran Enciclopedia Vasca, 1972.

Kardaberatz, Agustín. 1761. *Eusqueraren berri onac*. Reprinted in *Obras completas de Agustín de Kardaberaz* (i): 153–170. Bilbao: La Gran Enciclopedia Vasca, 1973.

Kardaberatz, Agustín. 1764. *Jesus, Maria, ta Joseren devociñoco Libruchoric atararico devociño batzuc*. Reprinted in *Obras completas de Agustín de Kardaberaz* (ii): 51–96. Bilbao: La Gran Enciclopedia Vasca, 1974.

Kardaberatz, Agustín. 1973. *Dotrina cristiana edo cristiñau dotrinea*. Reprinted in *Obras completas de Agustín de Kardaberaz* (i): 399–478. Bilbao: La Gran Enciclopedia Vasca.

Lacombe, Georges. 1924. "Langue basque". (A. Meillet and M. Cohen, eds.) *Les langues du monde*: 255–270. Second revised edition. Paris: Centre National de la Recherche Scientifique, 1952.

Lafitte, Pierre. 1944. *Grammaire basque (navarro-labourdin littéraire)*. Reprinted in Donostia: Elkar, 1979.

Lafon, René. 1944. *Le système du verbe basque au xviè siècle*. Reprinted in Donostia: Elkar, 1980.

Laka, Itziar. 1986–1987. "Hiperbizkaieraren historiaz". *Anuario del Seminario de Filología Vasca "Julio de Urquijo"*, 20–3: 705–754, 21–1: 13–40, 21–2: 409–424 and 21–3: 727–811. Donostia: Diputación Foral de Gipuzkoa.

Lakarra, Joseba Andoni. 1997. *Refranes y sentencias (1596). Ikerketak eta edizioa*. Bilbao: Real Academia de la Lengua Vasca.

Larramendi, Manuel. 1729. *El impossible vencido. Arte de la Lengua Bascongada*. Salamanca: Antonio Joseph Villagordo Alcaráz.

Larramendi, Manuel. 1745. *Diccionario trilingüe del castellano, bascuence y latín*. Donostia: Bartolomé Riesgo y Montero.

Madariaga, Bartolomé. 1828. *Plauto bascongado, ó el bascuence de Plauto en su comedia Pænulo, Acto 5º, Escena 1ª*. Reprinted in (J. A. Lakarra and B. Urgell, eds.) *Anuario del Seminario de Filología Vasca "Julio de Urquijo"*, 22–2: 494–519. Donostia: Diputación Foral de Gipuzkoa, 1988.

Materra, Esteve. 1617. *Dotrina christiana*. (D. Krajewska, E. Zuloaga, E. Santazilia, B. Ariztimuño, O. Uribe-Etxebarria and U. Reguero, eds.) *Esteve Materraren Do(c) trina Christiana (1617 & 1623)*. *Edizioa eta azterketa*. Bilbao: Real Academia de la Lengua Vasca and Universidad del País Vasco, 2017.

Mitxelena, Koldo. 1964. *Sobre el pasado de la lengua vasca*. Reprinted in *Sobre historia de la lengua vasca* (I): 1–73. *Anejos del Anuario del Seminario de Filología Vasca "Julio de Urquijo"*, nº 10. Donostia: Diputación Foral de Gipuzkoa, 1988.

Mitxelena, Koldo. 1981. "Lengua común y dialectos vascos". *Anuario del Seminario de Filología Vasca "Julio de Urquijo"*, 15: 289–313. Donostia: Diputación Foral de Gipuzkoa.

Mogel, Juan Antonio. 1800. *Confesio ta comunioco sacramentuen gañean eracasteac*. Iruña.

Mogel, Juan Antonio. 1803. *Confesino ona edo ceimbat gauzac lagundu biar deutseen Confesinuari ondo eguiña izateco*. Gasteiz.

Mogel, Juan Antonio. 1935. *La historia y geografía de España ilustradas por el idioma vascuence*. (J. Garate, ed.) *Euskera*, 16: 185–354. Bilbao: Academia de la Lengua Vasca.

Mokoroa, Justo (Ibar). 1936. *Genio y Lengua*. Tolosa: Librería de Mocoroa Hermanos.

Ormaetxea, Nikolas (Orixe). 1950. "Euskal aditza. Sarrera". *Euzko-Gogoa* 1, nº 5–6, 40–45. Guatemala.

Ormaetxea, Nikolas (Orixe). 1959. "*Mea culpa* eta *Quos ego!*". *Jakin*, nº 9, 89–93. Arantzazu-Oñati.

Ormaetxea, Nikolas (Orixe). 1961. "Itz gogorrak euskeraz. Abstracto, acción, acto". *Jakin*, nº 14, 30–34. Arantzazu-Oñati.

Oyharçabal, Beñat. 2001. "Zenbait gogoeta euskarak letra hizkuntza gisa izan duen bilakaeraz (XVII–XVIII. mendeak)". *Litterae Vasconicae*, nº 8, 9–46. Bilbao: Labayru Ikastegia.

Pagola, Inés. 2005. *Neologismos en la obra de Sabino Arana Goiri*. Bilbao: Real Academia de la Lengua Vasca.

Ruiz de Larrinaga, Juan (ed.). 1954–1958. "Cartas del P. Uriarte al Príncipe Luis Luciano Bonaparte". *Boletín de la Real Sociedad Vascongada de los Amigos del País*, 10: 231–302, 13: 220–239, 330–348, 429–452 and 14: 397–443. Donostia: Diputación Foral de Gipuzkoa.

Soloeta, Saturnino (Soloeta-Dima). 1922. *Ensayo de la unificación de dialectos baskos*. Buenos Aires: La Baskonia.

Tovar, Antonio. 1959. *El Euskera y sus parientes*. Madrid: Minotauro.

Uhlenbeck, Christianus Cornelis. 1947. "Les couches anciennes du vocabulaire basque". *Eusko-Jakintza*, 1: 543–581. Baiona: Musée Basque.

Villasante, Luis. (ed.). 1964. "Texto de dos impresos sumamente raros de Juan Antonio de Moguel". *Boletín de la Real Sociedad Vascongada de los Amigos del País*, 20: 61–73. Donostia: Diputación Foral de Gipuzkoa.

Zabala, Juan Mateo. 1848. *El verbo regular vascongado del dialecto vizcaino*. Donostia: Ignacio Ramón Baroja.

Zuazo, Koldo. 2017. *Mendebaleko euskara*. Donostia: Elkar.

6 The standardisation of Basque

I have often said in this book that the standardisation of Basque is something that has happened since 1964. It is a recent process, and not yet a finished one. Why the delay? One of the most important reasons for it is undoubtedly the message put out by Manuel Larramendi: that it would be best to use all dialects, since they are all equally good and perfect, and because they constitute an immense source of enrichment for the language. One result of this message was the formation of the five literary dialects discussed in the previous chapter, which, in the last analysis, hampered the creation of a single model, valid for all the Basques.

Beyond Larramendi's influence, one should not forget the special plight of Basque: as a marginalised language in the domains of administration and education, rarely consigned to writing, and existing alongside languages that had already been standardised (Latin, Occitan, Navarrese Romance, French, or Castilian), languages known by the ruling classes, who were, by definition, those who did the writing. Basque's dialectal division also stood in the way of efforts to unite it, in a vicious circle whereby dialectal division hampered standardisation and the lack of standardisation increased the division.

The standardisation of Basque passed through three distinct stages: the period before the twentieth century; the first half of the twentieth century; and the period since 1964, which will lead me to look at standard Basque as currently used (see also Hualde and Zuazo 2007).

The period before the twentieth century

In this period, two people played a key role in standardising Basque: Manuel Larramendi and Sabino Arana Goiri.

The legacy of Larramendi

Larramendi was opposed to standardising Basque and championed using all the dialects. How to use them? He suggested two solutions. On some occasions, he defended the idea that all Basques should give priority to their own dialect, but he also insisted that they should know other dialects too. On other occasions, he recommended the Greek example, that of choosing a dialect according to the literary genre it supposedly favoured. But despite proclaiming freedom in the use of dialects, he also mentioned a number of factors that in his view favoured Gipuzkoan. This is what he said in the prologue to his dictionary (Larramendi 1745: xxix):

> In the province [of Gipuzkoa] there is one dialect that, compared with the others, may be said to be the best, the most intelligible, and the most elegant, to which effect one could cite witnesses in the other dialects, who confess it to be a fact. This dialect is the only one that is everywhere surrounded by Basque territory (by Bizkaia, Araba, Navarre, and Lapurdi), and has therefore been able to preserve itself with the greatest degree of culture and splendour.[1]

Agustín Kardaberatz was in full agreement with Larramendi. In his *Eusqueraren berri onac*, he too defended the supremacy of the Gipuzkoan dialect. In his opinion, it was the most intelligible from the point of view of Basques as a whole (Kardaberatz 1761: 63):

> Our dialect, being in the middle of the other two, is the one best understood in Bizkaia and Navarre. For the Navarrese does not understand the Bizkaian nor the Bizkaian the Navarrese, while each marches for his own, at a great distance from the other.[2]

As I showed in the previous chapter, Juan Antonio Mogel, despite being a Bizkaian, wrote part of his work in the Gipuzkoan dialect. In the prologue to a work that remained unpublished until the late twentieth century, he explained that he based his decision to do so on the greater intelligibility of that dialect, as well as on the greater "taste" with which it was associated in Bizkaia and Navarre. In other words, Gipuzkoan was the most prestigious dialect south of the Pyrenees (Mogel 1987 [Villasante, ed.]: 88–89):

> Which of [the dialects] should be preferred I will not say, for it would displease more than one. I only know that Gipuzkoan is more affectionate, and has the advantage that both the Bizkaians and the Navarrese like to hear it, and understand it, while they do not understand each other.[3]

Bonaparte (1869 [1991]) also expressed his preference for Gipuzkoan: (422)

> I will take my examples mainly from the Gipuzkoan literary dialect, because it is the best known, the most widely spoken, the most cultured, one of the richest and most regular, and, as it were, the true representative of the Basque language, at more or less the same level as Tuscan and Castilian are in regard to the Italian language and Spanish.[4]

Apart from those in favour of the Gipuzkoan dialect, throughout the eighteenth and nineteenth centuries next to no further steps were taken towards the standardisation of Basque. The exception was, to a certain extent, Jose Francisco Aizkibel (1798–1864). This Gipuzkoan thought the time had come to set up an academy to carry out, among other things, the standardisation of the language. But this should be done only "to a certain extent," for it does not seem that his ideas had much traction in Basque society at the time. On the one hand, he spent most of his life outside the country; on the other, most of his writings remained for a long time unpublished. Whatever the case, here is what he wrote in the prologue to his Castilian-Basque dictionary, which was published in 1884, 20 years after his death (Aizkibel 1884: vi):

> An academy should be formed, composed of the most enlightened men of the Basque Country, both French and Spanish, for such is absolutely necessary for our language to advance, so that over time, by modifying the differences in spelling and pronunciation, and generalising without distinction words from the different dialects in writing and literature, a common language grows up, understandable in all provinces.[5]

To return to the prestige that the Gipuzkoan dialect was gaining, its success is easily detectable in the western part of Navarre, bordering on Gipuzkoa, and in the Deba Valley, which is administratively Gipuzkoan but, from the point of view of the language, closest to Bizkaian. The following two testimonies are from this region.

The first is from a letter written by the Franciscan friar José Antonio Uriarte to Prince Bonaparte in 1859. It describes the linguistic situation in the Deba Valley, where Uriarte was engaged in pastoral work (Ruiz de Larrinaga 1954: 276):

> All these places disdain the Basque of Bizkaia and are very passionate about the dialect of Beterri [in Gipuzkoa]: sermons and talks are conducted in the dialect of Beterri and many people learn this dialect, which they mix with their native dialect; but they have still not been able to *gipuzkoanise* the people.[6]

Two points in this fragment deserve attention. It was said, on the one hand, that people belonging to the highest social strata were careful to speak in the Gipuzkoan dialect, which did not usually happen in the Basque Country, since, generally speaking, that sector of society has used either French or Castilian or some other language, depending on which period we are talking about. I would also like to underline the word "disdain," used by Uriarte to refer to the way these people felt about their own dialect. Even Bonaparte expressed the same view in a letter written in 1863 to a collaborator of his. In it, he described the linguistic situation in Bergara, an important place in the Deba Valley, as follows (Urkijo 1908–1910 [1969]: 257):

When I say Bizkaian and not the Gipuzkoan of Bergara, I know perfectly well that this statement will displease the Bergarese, who boast of being pure Gipuzkoans. I am not unaware that the sermons of the most learned priests and often even the ordinary conversations of the best educated people are not only conducted in Gipuzkoan but even in its purest Beterri variety. But in spite of everything, my way of thinking remains the same. Leaving aside the fact that the gentlemen of Bergara may or may not like the Bizkaians and their dialect, the fact is that the Bergarese variety in use among the humble peasants belongs, from a linguistic point of view, to the Eastern Bizkaian dialect.[7]

Sabino Arana Goiri's position

Arana Goiri's standpoint was also decisive and still remains alive, especially in some sectors close to his party (the Basque Nationalists) in Bizkaia. One might think that the leader and founder of a political party that aspired to unify all the Basque provinces and to integrate them into a sovereign state would favour the creation of a common language for the citizens of that state, but such was not the case. Arana Goiri proposed a confederal project, in which each province would retain its own personality and characteristics, including in regard to language. This idea is expressed, for example, in Article 8 of the Draft Regulation of Bilbao's Euskaldun Batzokija ("Basque society"; Arana Goiri 1894 [1980]: 280):

> Bizkaia, related because of its race, language, faith, character, and customs to Araba, Lower Navarre, Gipuzkoa, Lapurdi, Navarre, and Zuberoa, will link or federate with these six peoples to form the whole called *Euskelerria* (Euskeria), but without any diminution of its autonomy. This doctrine is expressed in the following principle: *Free Bizkaia in Free Euskeria.* [8]

Thus, Arana Goiri breathed new life into Larramendi's thesis, and was wholly opposed to the standardisation of the language. In his view, standardisation was at variance with the essence of the Basque Country and would entail the loss of the riches found within the various dialects. He favoured the standardisation only of each individual dialect, to be achieved by giving priority to the oldest features conserved in each of them. He expounded these ideas in his work *Lecciones de ortografía del euskera bizkaino* ("Lessons in the spelling of Bizkaian Basque"; Arana Goiri 1896 [1980]: 822):

> In my opinion, it is necessary within each Euskerian region that has previously been an autonomous state, and might one day revert to being one, to compose a general dialect formed by elements less distant from the organic forms, scattered here and there, in the different subdialects or varieties spoken in the territory in question. [...] In this way, we would

have a single Gipuzkoan Basque, a single Navarrese Basque, a single Bizkaian Basque, and so on, thus realising in the linguistic sphere the formula that in the political sphere has so many and such staunch supporters, *variety in unity.* [9]

Orthographic normalisation

Before the twentieth century, despite the rejection of the idea of language standardisation, the desire for orthographic unification was accepted practically unanimously. However, here too there was an important disagreement about the area to which such rules would apply. Some limited them to the Basque provinces of the French state, others to those of the Spanish state. For example, the norms proposed by Agustín Kardaberatz (1761) in *Eusqueraren berri onac* did not take the phonological peculiarities of the northern dialects into account.

The Lapurdian priest Martin Duhalde, in a work published in 1809, decided to depart from the orthographic norms of the French language and to use other, simpler ones that were more in line with the structure of Basque (Duhalde 1809). The reform initiated by Duhalde was taken further by another priest, Jean-Pierre Darrigol, also a Lapurdian, in a grammatical work titled *Dissertation critique et apologétique sur la langue basque* ("Critical and apologetic dissertation on the Basque language"), published, it would seem, in 1827 (Darrigol 1827). In summary, he proposed the following changes:

1   Always write *g*, without distinguishing between *g* and *gu*.
2   Write *k*, and do away with *c* and *qu*.
3   Write *z*, and do away with *c* and *ç*.
4   Write *i*, and do away with *y*.
5   Always write *b*, and do away with *v*.

All these reforms were accepted in the work *Andre-dena Mariaren ilhabethea* ("The month of the Virgin Mary"), written, apparently, by the Lapurdian priest Jean Jauretxe (1838), and also in *Études grammaticales sur la langue euskarienne* ("Grammatical studies on the Euskarian language"), by Antoine d'Abbadie and Augustin Chaho, the first grammar of the Zuberoan dialect, published in 1836 (d'Abbadie and Chaho 1836). This latter work also proposed replacing grapheme *x* with *ts*, to signify the sound / ts /.

The well-known Zuberoan journalist and writer Augustin Chaho (1810–1858) played a decisive role in the diffusion of the new norms. He took care to ensure that they spread to the whole country. He said in the Baiona newspaper *Ariel*, on February 16, 1845:

We will try to demonstrate that all Basque books printed up to now are wrongly spelt, using an orthography alien to the Basque language. The one we propose can be applied to all the Basque dialects, and we would like to emphasise its judiciousness and rationality. In the absence of a norm-bestowing academy, churchmen and the educated citizenry, if they had a minimum of patriotism, should agree to put an end to the chaos that reigns in this field of our national literature.[10]

Then there is this further note published in *Ariel*, on September 28, 1845:

> The spelling of Basque texts that we publish is criticised rather frivolously by those people who fail to understand our goal. It is a matter of following orthographic rules that are most adequate for all the Basque dialects. Some correspondents have given us their ideas on this subject, but we note that the majority, scarcely versed in our national literature, seem to ignore the system used in the Spanish provinces. They care only for the routine followed in the printing of books of piety in the Lapurdian dialect.[11]

As the latter text suggests, and as is natural and logical, the new orthographic norms were not immediately accepted. Apparently, the main resistance came from a section of the Church. The writer Jean Duvoisin explained the situation to Prince Bonaparte, in a letter written in 1869, as follows (Daranatz 1928-1931 [1972]: 164):

> The clergy has not yet decided to accept the reform in their little Church books, because of a fear – hardly justified – that it will not be welcome.[12]

In another manuscript, Duvoisin refers to the priest Jauretxe, whom we have already met, and his work *Andre-dena Mariaren ilhabethea*, which used the new norms. The said sector of the Church supposedly reacted as follows (Altuna 1987: 84–85):

> The priest Jauretxe was the first to realise that the spelling was defective. In his *Month of Mary* he included a brief explanation, full of correct observations, and although he dared not break with the dominant habits, he introduced at least some reforms into his books. He became the object of ruthless criticism. They attacked him from all sides and even got Monsignor the bishop to intervene, to force Jauretxe to retreat. This good man, very humble, perfectly distinguished black from white, but nevertheless he had to make some concessions against his will and was only then able to publish his book.[13]

Apparently, it was Prince Bonaparte's intervention that tipped the balance in favour of reform. Duvoisin confessed as much, in a letter to the Gipuzkoan writer Antonio Arzak in 1885 (Daranatz 1928-1931 [1972]: 332–333):

> Until Prince Louis-Lucien was among us, each wrote Basque in his own way, although the differences were not great and, in fact, it was easy to

reach an agreement. The prince took care of it, using his status as a great philologist. From then on, the spelling became rational and writers accepted it immediately.[14]

Prince Bonaparte's great prestige meant that reform finally reached the southern provinces, where until then people had continued writing according to the rules of Castilian. Among the first to adopt the new norms was the Bilbaoan Luis Iza (1837–1892). In the "Preliminary Notice" to the Basque version of Calderón de la Barca's *The Mayor of Zalamea*, he said (Iza 1881):

> Although there is still no language academy among us, most of what we have written in Basque adopts, as most in accord with its nature, the spelling recognised and taught by my enlightened and generous teacher, who on account of many illustrious merits is Prince Louis Lucien Bonaparte. The *v* is unknown in our alphabet, so we use only the *b*. *K* is used in place of *c* and *qu*. We use *g* in the case of *ge* and *gi*, with the same sound as in *ga, go,* and *gu. H* is unused because it is considered useless. We write *z* instead of *c* before *e* and *i*. Before *b* and *p* we use *n* instead of *m*, just as we use *rr* in all cases of strong sound, bearing in mind that it never appears as an initial, unless preceded by an *e* for the purposes of euphony.[15]

José Manterola (1880), in his *Cancionero vasco* ("Basque songbook"; XIII–XXI), like Arturo Campión (1880), in his *Gramática euskara* ("Basque grammar"; 1880: 5–8), accepted the new orthographic system, which soon spread throughout the Basque Country. The biggest problem concerned *h*. The aspirated sound was still alive in most of the northern provinces, so that *h* was part of their orthographic system. In the southern provinces, where there was no aspiration, it was considered superfluous.

At the end of the nineteenth century, the orthographic question awakened a keen interest in the southern provinces, and two extensive treatises on the subject appeared in print. They were the work of Resurrección María Azkue and Sabino Arana Goiri. Both studies were published in 1896 (Azkue 1896, Arana Goiri 1896)

The main novelty was the substitution of single letters to which accents would be added for double letters. In other words, *d́, ĺ, ŕ,* and *t́* would replace *dd, ll, rr,* and *tt*. In fact, the use of accents was not entirely new, since Jose Francisco Aizkibel had already made use of them in his dictionary published in 1884. They were also mentioned in the works on spelling by the Jesuit José Ignacio Arana (1872, 1895). Sabino Arana Goiri also proposed using *x* and *tx* for the sounds /ʃ/ and /tʃ/, as in Catalan, sounds that in Basque were written in different ways.

All these reforms, proposed by Azkue and Arana Goiri, despite their novelty and exoticism, quickly took root in the southern provinces. Their success was probably due to the influence that Sabino Arana Goiri exercised over his party's members and supporters, at a time when the Basque Country found itself in difficulties in the wake of the Second Carlist War.

The standardisation of Basque in the first half of the twentieth century

In the twentieth century, two important events took place. Starting in 1910, the review *Euzkadi* ran an information campaign on the question of the standardisation of Basque; and in 1918, the Basque Language Academy was established, and decided to take the reins of that process.

Euzkadi's *information campaign*

In 1910 *Euzkadi*, published in Bilbao, started a debate on the standardisation of Basque, under the title "The question of the dialects." *Euzkadi* was the bulletin of the Basque Nationalist Party, which up to then had opposed standardisation, in line with the guidelines established by its leader, Sabino Arana Goiri.

In its presentation of the debate, it invited the participation of "the largest possible number of Basquophiles, regardless of party or school," and posed four questions in an attempt to focus the debate. They were (Euzkadi 1910):

1   Would it be right to aim for the uniformity of this language, at least at the literary level?
2   Should this uniformity be absolute, as far as possible, or should it be limited to one or more elements of the language, such as phonetics or lexicon?
3   What means might be used to realise the homogeneity of literary Basque? Could it be done by means of an agreement between all Basque Euzkerists, or would it be necessary to proceed by way of a slow evolution of the present literary forms?
4   Would homogeneous literary Basque be one of the dialects currently preferred over the others, although with grammatical elements taken from all them, or would it be a language that was to a certain extent new, formed with elements of all the dialects but without any one of them exercising a preponderant influence?[16]

Most of those who participated in the debate favoured standardisation, and opinions were even voiced that were radically opposed to those previously defended, opinions that came from no less a place than the ranks of the Basque Nationalist Party itself. Koldobika Eleizalde, for example, expressed his complete disagreement with the principles elaborated by Sabino Arana Goiri (Eleizalde 1911):

I cannot agree in this regard with the great patriotic writer. If there has to be one Basque for Gipuzkoa, another for Navarre, another for Bizkaia, etc., any Basque literature will be impossible: it is purely a matter of fact, and there is no need for a demonstration of it. [...] I think that the general aspiration today is in the direction of uniformity, at least for literary Basque.[17]

Ikabalzeta, for his part, who was prepared to adopt the Gipuzkoan dialect as a basis for standardisation, thus detached himself from the nationalist nucleus in Bilbao, which favoured giving preference to the Bizkaian dialect (Ikabalzeta 1910):

> For me, unification on the basis of the Gipuzkoan dialect, adopted from now on as literary, is the most practical solution: Gipuzkoan is a living dialect, spoken by more people than any other, it is the most central, the most similar to the rest, and the one with greater influence on the rest; I also understand that, from a literary point of view, it is and always was the most cultivated. It should be noted that I am not a Gipuzkoan, and I have no known Gipuzkoan descent; but it seems to me that no dialect can dispute its primacy.[18]

In the new atmosphere generated by this debate, new reflections on the theme of standardisation began to appear in following years. Interventions by Koldobika Eleizalde (1919a, 1919b) and Federico Belaustegigoitia (1916) remain, in my opinion, fully valid right up to the present time. Both Eleizalde and Belaustegigoitia were members of the Basque Nationalist Party.

Eleizalde (1919a) objected to the extreme advocates of the dialects, who saw them as a treasure to be preserved above all else (37):

> We will need to solve the question of the dialects. [...] To imagine that a small country of half a million souls, almost all of them illiterate, little given to reading, can afford the indulgence of three or four literary dialects is tantamount to denying any possibility of Basque culturality. These three or four literary dialects will serve only to write an eloquent epitaph to the common language, an unhappy victim of such nefarious luxuries. [...] I now recognise that the literary renaissance of the language is absolutely conditional on the adoption of a single and uniform dialect for the written and even for the oral literary language.[19]

Eleizalde was not deceived by false myths and was aware of the causes and consequences of the linguistic diversity:

> This diversity of dialects, subdialects and varieties has been maintained by two main circumstances, the lack of a traditional written literature and the unhappy political division in which the Basque nation has lived throughout its history.[20]

Among the interesting and sensible reflections of Federico Belaustegigoitia (1877–1947) is his allusion to the need for a standardised language that could be learned by people ignorant of Basque. This was precisely his own case (Belaustegigoitia 1916: 1):

> The study of Basque for those who are not native speakers of it is, precisely because of the diversity of dialects and subdialects, incomparably pointless and unrewarding; what they learn to hear and say will be of use only in a handful of villages, unless they make new efforts.[21]

Belaustegigoitia, although born in Araba and a resident of Durango (Bizkaia), was in favour of adopting the Gipuzkoan dialect. To the usual arguments (greater intelligibility, greater prestige, rich literary tradition), he added the following two: Basque was kept alive in important parts of Gipuzkoa, which favoured its diffusion, and in those places people of high social status used Basque (Belaustegigoitia 1916: 17):

> Comparing dialects one to the others, we will have of course to discard the *Zuberoan*, an extreme variety of language, just as its territory is extreme and bereft of communication with the rest of the country, and the same will have to go for *Lapurdian*, despite its greater affinity with the Peninsular dialects; this affinity is greatly impaired by the French invasion, the lack of centres of Basque life, and, in short, the evident lack of influence of Lapurdian Basque on the others. [...] With the question of primacy reduced to just Bizkaian and Vascon (or Gipuzkoan) Basque, it must be conceded that most of the advantages lie with the latter. The number of inhabitants that currently speak Bizkaian is not comparable to that of Basques who speak Gipuzkoan; the quality of the population, almost all them labourers or fisherman in Bizkaia; and the status of the towns or villages in which Bizkaian is spoken.[22]

Although the arguments in favour of standardisation were consistent and sensible, and although their defenders were people of prestige and standing within the ranks of the Basque Nationalist Party, the party apparatus was opposed. In 1916, a booklet titled *Sobre la unificación del euzkera* ("On the unification of Basque") was published under the authorship of the Euzkeltzale-Bazkuna ("Basque centre"), where many of Sabino Arana Goiri's ideas were repeated. They gave three fundamental reasons for their opposition to standardisation:

a   The dialect differences were small and would disappear once Basque language acquired a role in education.
b   Standardisation would result in the loss of much of the wealth contained in each of the dialects.
c   The adoption of any one dialect as the basis for standardisation would resurrect old rivalries among speakers and would at the same time mean that people from other dialect areas would have to learn it.

According to this view, the weakness of Basque was not the lack of a standard model or even its minimal use in literature but the lack of true patriotism. That was where work needed to be done (Euzkeltzale-Bazkuna 1916):

> Living languages exist without the least vestige of literature. The known history of Basque is the history of a language that in the course of long centuries has not produced an appreciable literature. Is that why it is on the point of death? No, it has reached that point because of the lack of true national consciousness, of true patriotism (p. 22).
>
> To attribute the death of Basque to the diversity of its dialects is to beat about the bush. To claim to be able to avoid that death by means of the disappearance of those dialects is to seek to cure the disease by applying medicine to the healthy part and not to the sick. We say with the Master [Sabino Arana Goiri] once and for all: Basque for Basque's sake has no future; Basque for the country's sake will endure (p. 61).[23]

Contrary to what is generally thought, they did not at all agree to base standard Basque on the Gipuzkoan dialect. The dialect chosen would have to be Bizkaian, for it was the richest and oldest:

> It follows that by means of comparative study of the dialects Sabino [Arana Goiri] showed that Bizkaian is the closest to primitive Basque, the most uniform, the richest in phonetics and in the verb, and the most radically postpositive (p. 12).[24]

These arguments are odd. Apart from the difficulty of proving which is the most primitive, the richest, and the most postpositive dialect, when elaborating a model for a standard language one must give priority to other factors, such as the number of speakers, the dialect's prestige and intelligibility, the infrastructure available for its later diffusion, and so on.

In short, the Euzkeltzale-Bazkuna Basque Centre only accepted standardisation of the language's spelling and its newly coined words. Apart from that, it was also in favour of each dialect's internal standardisation. So, it remained faithful to the views expressed by Sabino Arana Goiri a few years before.

The intervention of the Academy of the Basque Language

Given the impossibility of reaching an accord, the best solution was thought to be the founding of an Academy of the Language. It was constituted in 1918, under the patronage of the councils of Araba, Bizkaia, Gipuzkoa, and Navarre. Naturally, one of the prime objectives was to create a standard language, and two members, the Navarrese Arturo

Campión and the Lapurdian Pierre Broussain, were charged with drawing up a document to address this question.

Their "Report" was ready by 1920 (Campión and Broussain 1922). The authors considered standardisation to be a matter of urgency, but they did not present a clear proposal for how to go about it. They emphasised the importance that Gipuzkoan had acquired over the last few centuries and the past greatness of Lapurdian. In their opinion, the standard language would have to be based on one of those dialects or, perhaps, the result of a synthesis of the two.

The Academy quickly organised four days of debate, in the years 1920 and 1921, to discuss the project. The meeting drew a wide response. Sixteen papers were presented and, outside the ambit of the Academy itself, several articles were published on the same topic.

Among the 16 papers presented within the Academy, only one supported Campion and Broussain's approach. This is not surprising, given its lack of precision. The remaining 15 papers can be classed as follows (Euskaltzaindia 1922):

a   Against standardisation: 5.
b   For the "reconstruction of the original Basque": 1.
c   For the Bizkaian dialect: 1.
d   For the Gipuzkoan dialect: 4.
e   For "enriched Gipuzcoan": 2.
f   For "enriched Basque": 2.

As can be appreciated, the outlook was frankly bleak. Given that the strategies for tackling standardisation were so disparate, any kind of agreement was ruled out. There were proposals that did not reach the minimum degree of common sense. It was unthinkable, for example, that Bizkaian, the dialect furthest removed from the rest, could serve as an ideal basis for standardisation. The reasons put forward by those who supported it were also inappropriate. They emphasised its supposedly greater antiquity, wealth, and regularity.

In the previous chapter, I mentioned the preposterous proposal to reconstruct Basque as spoken by primitive Basques. On this occasion, it was the Capuchin friar Iñaki Ayengiz who defended this road to standardisation.

Although it might at first sight seem a good idea to form a standard Basque by mixing together all the dialects ("enriched Basque"), the result could only be a wholly artificial language, acceptable to the speakers of none of the dialects, all of whom would see it as alien and exotic. The same went, but to a lesser extent, for "enriched Gipuzkoan," which we will discuss in greater detail shortly.

But beyond the dispersion and disparity of ideas among supporters of standardisation, there were others who opposed the project *tout court*. Among them, the most solid and compact group was formed by officials of the Basque Nationalist Party in Bilbao, whose ideas were defended to the Academy by

Manuel Egileor. Actually, he merely sent a copy of the booklet edited by Euzkeltzale-Bazkuna in 1916.

The writer Nikolas Ormaetxea *Orixe*, the Spanish philologist Ramón Menéndez Pidal, and the professor and essayist Miguel Unamuno were all opposed to standardisation and, being so influential, are especially relevant to the debate.

Ormaetxea (1920) said little that was new. In his view, adopting a single dialect as the basis of standardisation would be harmful in four ways (54):

a   It would impoverish the grammar.
b   It would lead to a lack of freshness and spontaneity in writing.
c   It would mean not being able to profit to the same extent from a literary point of view as one might if the rest participated.
d   It would wound the *amour propre* of those who saw their own dialect relegated.

Nor was the solution he proposed new. It was no different from the one Larramendi had put forward two centuries earlier: to allow writers the freedom to choose, according to the literary genre in which they were writing, the dialect deemed most appropriate, following the model of ancient Greece (Ormaetxea 1920 [1969]: 58–59):

> If Demosthenes or Pindar had to write in Aitor's language today,[25] they would choose one dialect for their harangues and another one for their passionate odes: the dry Bizkaian dialect, or they would take from it the largest dose, seasoning their language with elements of other dialects on a minor scale; Lysias, Socrates, or Cicero would, I imagine, take Gipuzkoan as their base; finally, Anacreonte, Lucian the philosopher, or Aristophanes, with their elegant and satirical essays, would find no better base than Pyrenean. [...] That is the norm that seems to me the best to follow, and none so apt to realise it as the writers themselves.[26]

The lecture Menéndez Pidal gave in Bilbao in 1920 produced a strong and favourable impression. He had the mistaken idea that standardisation would necessarily result in the creation of a new, artificial language. No wonder, then, that he was against it. But as well as opposing standardisation, he raised questions of a different nature, in assigning the following functions to Basque: oral use in the domestic and colloquial spheres, and assisting scientists and researchers of the past. The cultural and literary domains were reserved for French and Castilian (Menéndez Pidal 1920 [1962]: 53–54):

> Let us assume that [the standardisation of Basque], which I consider impossible, could be realised, and that new generations of Basques will learn the unified artificial language. The Academy, instead of continuing, purifying, and promoting historical Basque, as is its mission, would have

abruptly broken with tradition in its development of the language, and launched it in a new direction; it would have deprived the language of the greater part of its value and historic authority; it would have killed off the venerable dialects, consecrated by the fervent devotion of generations of Basques over many centuries; and it would have sacrificed them for a new product, devoid of archaeological interest and of no use whatsoever for human culture, created for the sole puerile purpose of being able to say in an exotic language what can be said to great effect in either of the two great cultural languages of the western extremity of Europe.[27]

The position of Miguel Unamuno (1920 [1958]) was, as usual, much more extreme. He even denied Basque the capacity for evolution and development that every language has (347):

> In Basque you cannot think with universality. And the Basque people, when it rises to universality, does so in Castilian or French. [...] The authors of the Report [Campion and Broussain] know and acknowledge the inability of living Basque to express in all their fullness the multiple aspects of modern life; they know full well that one cannot explain chemistry, physics, psychology, or ... any science in Basque. They know full well that the religious, theological, and psychological vocabulary of Basque is of Latin origin.[28]

Azkue's "enriched Gipuzkoan"

Given the meagre outcome of the conference discussion, the Academy of the Basque Language found itself powerless to continue the standardisation project. Quite apart from the lack of external support, there was no clear evidence within the Academy itself of any evident desire to achieve such an aim. As José Luis Alvarez Enparantza (1994: 132–133), known as *Txillardegi*, recalls, several of its members were unable to express themselves in Basque, and the academic sessions were held until 1951 in Castilian. It was Federico Krutwig, who had learned Basque as an adolescent, who requested that they be held in Basque. Some academics continued to write in Castilian and, according to Alvarez Enparantza, often conducted their relations with one another in French or Castilian. So, it is understandable that a team of people with these characteristics would not resolve to face up to such an arduous undertaking as the standardisation of the language.

Faced with this state of affairs, Resurrección María Azkue, President of the Academy, continued working by himself on an old project: *gipuzkera osotua*, or "enriched Gipuzkoan." As the name suggests, it was a question of adopting the Gipuzkoan dialect as the basis of standardisation but adorning it with bits and pieces from the other dialects.

Azkue's aim was to take full advantage of the circumstances that worked in favour of Gipuzkoan (its vitality and greater intelligibility) and, at the same time, to avoid the evils that standardisation would supposedly bring in its wake, which, in the view of most, were:

a   The loss of the riches distributed across the various dialects.
b   Resistance by non-Gipuzkoan speakers.
c   The generation of a feeling of inferiority on the part of non-Gipuzkoan speakers.

Azkue favoured Gipuzkoan despite being a Bizkaian, and many Bizkaians followed him. His project failed to take root, for three main reasons.

1   Azkue and his followers were unable to achieve their aim of getting others to assist, each in his or her own way, in the enrichment of Gipuzkoan, in accordance with their wishes and competencies. Far from constituting a project to standardise the language, it turned out to be the very opposite. The theoretical works Azkue wrote as part of an attempt to create a structure for his model, *Prontuario fácil para el estudio de la lengua vasca* ("Simple handbook for the study of the Basque language"; Azkue 1917) and *Gipuzkera osotua* ("Enriched Gipuzkoan"; Azkue 1934–1935), as well as the practical example of his novel *Ardi Galdua* ("The stray sheep"; Azkue 1918), were insufficiently explicit. Moreover, Azkue lacked a homogeneous and compact group of collaborators. They all acted according to their own lights, guided more or less by their own instinct.
2   They failed to take into account the literary tradition and the past of the language, thus absorbing numerous local forms and expressions and innovations of recent coinage. This led to dispersion rather than to unification.
3   The Gipuzkoan writers who claimed to follow Azkue did not fully understand the true meaning of "enriched Gipuzkoan" and instead used "pure Gipuzkoan," which was ultimately the speech of their own locality or region.

This attitude on the part of the Gipuzkoans exasperated some Bizkaians and led them to abandon the project once and for all. A good example of this can be found in the testimony of Andima Ibiñagabeitia, tireless promoter of Basque and a supporter of Azkue's "enriched Gipuzkoan" (Ibiñagabeitia 1952: 239):

> I would like to give a warning to Gipuzkoan speakers. It is they who have been most sectarian. The Academy decided long ago to use verbal inflections of the type *dut* ("I have") instead of *det* [Gipuzkoan] or *dot* [western]. However, the Gipuzkoans still do not conform to the instruction and show no sign of abandoning their beloved *det*. Gentlemen, you too will have to yield on some points if we are to achieve the desired end. We have had to make greater and more painful concessions to strengthen and give encouragement to your beautiful dialect.[29]

Other Bizkaian writers made similar criticisms and, in the wake of these events, José Basterretxea Oskillaso, also a Bizkaian, came up with an alternative model for standardisation: *Euskara osotua*, or "enriched Basque." Basterretxea aimed to expand beyond the narrow framework of the Gipuzkoan dialect and to construct a Basque language in which all dialects could be accommodated equally, without granting predominance to any one of them. He put his model into practice in the novel *Kurloiak* ("Sparrows"; Basterretxea 1962).

The result was a totally exotic and artificial language, complete chaos, in which elements from all the dialects jostled one another without order or concert. This was pointed out by Koldo Mitxelena (1962) and Luis Villasante (1963), in reviews. Apart from a handful of Bizkaian writers or at least writers who used Bizkaian, like Jokin Zaitegi and Balendin Aurre-Apraiz, the model won no support.

I should add that when the Academy of the Basque Language came out in defence of the current model of standard Basque, some groups wanted to relaunch Azkue's "enriched Gipuzkoan." They included Euskerazaintza ("Basque academy"), a body parallel to the Academy of the Basque Language, created in 1978.

Euskara batua, standard Basque

I mentioned in the first chapter that from 1960 onwards, a series of historic changes began in the Basque Country. The main change was probably the creation of the *ikastola*, Basque-language schools for children and young people. Supporters of the *ikastola* movement were to the fore in pushing for the implementation of a standard language that they could use in their textbooks and in other materials.

Also decisive was the intervention of a large group of Basque writers who wanted their works to reach all corners of the country, so that their work would become financially viable.

The actions of people who had learned Basque in their youth was another determining factor. Their main reason for learning Basque was so that they would be able to communicate in it, so it was logical that they should seek a suitable instrument to realise their goal, a type of language that would transcend the ubiquitous dialect barriers.

An increasingly broad political and social movement struggled to break free from the suffocating framework imposed by Franco's military dictatorship. Under Franco, it was impossible in many domains and circumstances to speak Basque normally or to correspond or publish in it. The concept of "race" had already lost the importance accorded to it in the late nineteenth century. Language once again came to occupy a central position in the new Basque Country that Basques yearned to bring into being. In the rest of this chapter, before concluding, I will describe the seven principal milestones that mark the progress towards a standard Basque language.

Gabriel Aresti's poem Maldan Behera ("Downhill"; 1959)

In 1959, a long poem by Gabriel Aresti (1933–1975), titled "Maldan Behera" (Aresti 1959), won a competition organised by the Academy of the Basque Language. Despite this recognition, the poem cannot be said to have had much impact, except that it was written in a language very similar to the one that, nine years later, would be promulgated under the name Euskara Batua, "standard Basque."

Its author, a native and resident of an almost totally Castilianised Bilbao, had learned Basque during his youth, outside his family environment. He never managed to speak Basque fluently, but he had an exceptional knowledge of it, both old and contemporary Basque, and of all its dialects and registers. Added to that, he had a fine linguistic intuition, so he was able to make adequate use of his deep acquaintance with the language. During the gestation of standard Basque, right up until his premature death in 1975, Gabriel Aresti played a key role.

The Euskal Idazkaritza Association of Baiona (1963–1964)

In 1963 the Euskal Idazkaritza ("Basque secretariat") was set up in Baiona, with a section in charge of language issues. It consisted of only a handful of people, but it represented a broad spectrum of Basque society: from north and south of the Basque Country, from the Church, and from various political organisations and parties. Again, its main motor was someone who had learned Basque in his youth: José Luis Alvarez Enparantza *Txillardegi*, from Donostia.

After eight months of weekly meetings, plans for standardisation were laid, and these were presented in August 1964 at a public meeting in Baiona. Most of those in attendance were teachers and writers. The meeting adopted the first norms of the current standard language model.

The document, only seven pages long, was made known to Basque society through the pages of the journal *Jakin*: "Baionako Biltzarraren Erabakiak" ("Resolutions of the Baiona Assembly"; Jakin 1965). It was divided into three sections: spelling, declension, and the verb.

a   *Spelling*. The meeting gave the go-ahead to the rules approved by the Academy of the Basque Language in the post-war period. The letters *j, x, tx, rr, ll, ñ,* and *dd* were therefore accepted. One innovation was introduced, the use of *h*, typical of the northern dialects. It was decided that it would be used, at first, between two vowels (e.g., *mihi*, "tongue") and to distinguish words spelt the same but with different meanings (*hura* "that," *ura* "water"). A list was issued of 82 basic words that would be written with *h*, with a warning that more would follow.

However, the use of *h* after the consonant groups *ph, th, kh, lh, nh, ñh,* and *rh* was ruled out. The reason for this decision has never been explained, since aspiration is documented in these consonant groups even on epigraphs from Roman times. It was probably because it was thought that speakers south of the Pyrenees would find it hard to accept and learn this feature. It was a wise decision, although it might also have been wise to allow its use in the province of Zuberoa, where aspiration continues to be pronounced in this context.

b   *Declension.* This section contained no major divergences in the designation of cases. The principal innovation was the adoption of the morpheme *-ek* in the ergative* plural, typical of central-eastern speech. Special attention was drawn to the correct use of words ending in *-a*, which caused much confusion in central-eastern dialects: *gauza* ("thing"), for example, instead of *gauz*.

c   *The verb.* This section dealt with the present and past verbal inflections of the Basque versions of the auxiliary verbs "to be" and "to have." Among the former inflections, the central forms of the type *naiz* ("I am") were adopted, rather than the western *naz* and the eastern *niz*, and among the latter inflections, the *dut* ("I have") type rather than the western *dot* and the Gipuzkoan *det*. Among the plural inflections of the Basque verb "to be," the document opted for the Gipuzkoan inflections with the root *-e: zera* ("you are"), *gera* ("we are"), and *zerate* ("you [plural] are") were to be accepted but were later replaced by inflections that had *-a* in the root (*zara, gara, zarete*).

The Idazleen Alkartea association ("Writers' association"; 1968)

In June 1968, the Gerediaga cultural association in the Durango region of Bizkaia organised an assembly in Ermua, aimed at giving fresh impetus to standardisation. The assembly agreed to comply strictly with the norms adopted in Baiona, together with some new ones. It published its resolutions in the journal *Jakin* (1968, nos 31–32, 15–74). The assembly also agreed to set up a writers' association, Idazleen Alkartea, which subsequently took up the reins of standardisation. It was this association that asked the Academy of the Basque Language to make room for a discussion of the question of standardisation in the programme of activities planned for the celebration of its fiftieth anniversary.

The Congress of the Academy of the Basque Language in Arantzazu (1968)

Under pressure from the Writers' Association and Basque society in general, the Academy of the Basque Language was forced to do as the association asked. The Academy charged one of its members, Koldo Mitxelena, with drawing up a discussion document.

The role played by Mitxelena (1915–1987) proved to be clincing. A trained linguist, he was perfectly at home in Basque, and fully abreast of the research that was being done outside the Basque Country. Within the Basque Country, his prestige was enormous and his authority unimpeachable. He was also aware of what had been done up to then in regard to standardisation.

Mitxelena presented plans to adopt the Gipuzkoan dialect as the basis for standardisation, in line the trend that had been developing ever since the eighteenth century. The reasons were as follows:

a   *Linguistic.* The Gipuzkoan dialect had become the best known and most easily understood of all Basque dialects.
b   *Demolinguistic.* The Gipuzkoan dialect, together with the western dialect, had the greatest number of speakers.
c   *Sociolinguistic.* The Gipuzkoan dialect was the most prestigious at that time, and the most used by writers. Ordinary speakers deemed that the Basque of Tolosa (an important Gipuzkoan centre) was the most elegant and tasteful form of the language.
d   *Socioeconomic.* Gipuzkoa had several important population centres with a large number of Basque speakers. They included Donostia (San Sebastián), Lezo-Pasaia-Errenteria, Hernani-Andoain-Lasarte-Usurbil, Tolosa, Ordizia-Beasain, Legazpi-Zumarraga-Urretxu, Azkoitia-Azpeitia, Zumaia-Zestoa, and Orio-Zarautz-Getaria. Irun-Hondarribia-Oiartzun, Arrasate-Oñati-Aretxabaleta-Eskoriatza, Bergara-Antzuola-Elgeta, and Eibar-Soraluze-Elgoibar are also demographically important, although the dialects spoken in these places are somewhat different from that spoken in the places mentioned.

But although he based his plans on Gipuzkoan, Mitxelena did not ignore the literary tradition, especially that of the seventeenth-century Lapurdian coast. He thus sought to minimise the influence of localisms and recent innovations, which would have presented new barriers to speakers.

Mitxelena's paper had three main pillars: declension, lexicon, and spelling. It was published, together with conference interventions, in the Academy's bulletin, *Euskera* (Euskaltzaindia 1968). It included a long list of words, which formed the initial outline for a dictionary of standard Basque.

The activities of the Academy between 1968 and 1978

The years following the Arantzazu Congress were years of enormous tension during which Basque society split into two. The standardisation of the language coincided with a process of change within Basque and world society, affecting all fields: religion, politics, economic structure, customs, and culture. By that very fact, all these questions often appeared to be mixed up together, even where they were not. Whatever the case, most members of younger generations favoured standardisation, while older people, especially those whose use of Basque was limited to the oral and colloquial sphere, were against.

The issue on which the two sides went to war, as a sort of proxy, boiled down to one single letter, *h*. As we have already seen, in southern dialects aspiration had been lost even before the sixteenth century, so it had never been used in writing. (The first book in Basque was not published until 1545.) In the northern dialects, on the other hand, aspiration had remained alive and was commonly used in writing.

To achieve standardisation of the language, there was no alternative other than either to accept or to reject *h*, but either choice would provoke discontent and disapproval in one or the other camp. After the Baiona Assembly in 1964, and even before then, some people in the southern Basque Country used the letter, and for two reasons. First, because in the past aspiration had been common to all dialects; second, because the loss of aspiration had thrown the pronunciation of many words into disarray. For example, *aho* ("mouth") was spoken and written as *abo, ago, ao*, or *aba*, according to which dialect was being spoken. Many thought that the solution lay in returning to the original common form *aho*, still alive in the northern dialects.

It was around that single letter that most of the controversy revolved. Arguing against standardisation was Antonio M. Labayen (1972), a well-known Basque cultural figure, who said (28–29):

> From the authors' own mouths, we know that they took the *h* as a symbol of their intentions, which are to destroy the cultural work realised in the course of the previous fifty years.[30] And above all, in whatever is traditional and consonant with the religious faith of our elders; under-mining their ways of life, their customs, and their family organisation. It is hatred of Christianity and not the conscience of a just socialism that impels them forward in their theoretical-revolutionary obsession, IRAULTZA! ["Revolution!"] against the negation of the values embodied in the moral and spiritual treasure of our people. One has only to read the books and pamphlets that they publish in their series; the articles in their newspapers and magazines, plagued in almost all cases with obscenities and Marxistoid phraseology. And all this under cover of *"batasuna"* ["unification"] and a profusion of aiches.[31]

Josu Arenaza (1974) was even more radical:

> The *h* is a political symbol, although it is denied by very learned gentle-men invested with seraphic habits. As political as the hammer and sickle or the swastika or both at once (pp. 84–85).
>
> Aichist spelling is no more nor less than an attempt to politicise Basque, breaking the traditional molds, as mere extensions of what they are actually intent on breaking: family, the right to a Christian education, our special customs, our personality, etc., as a means to achieve a youth without morality, without feelings, without an awareness of belonging to a people with customs are perhaps debatable but undoubtedly superior to those that they propose that we judge on the basis of the samples that we see (page 93).[32]

Apart from the *h*, the spelling of the palatal sounds also generated con-troversy. The Academy decided that the palatal sounds produced as a result of contact with the vowel *i* would not be reflected in writing, so that *il, in,* and *it* would replace *ill, iñ,* or *itt*, in words like *langile* ("worker"), *mina* ("pain"), or *iturri* ("source"). The reason for the decision was that these sounds are the product of an innovation that affects some but not all dialects, although among those affected are the two most widely spoken, the western and the central. However, even in those speeches in which change has occurred, the change is not always present with the same intensity, and there is much variation from one dialect to the other.

It is hard to fault the Academy's resolution, which said that palatalisations of this sort should not be reflected in writing and that speakers should be free to pronounce them according to the norms of their own speech community. However, the decision provoked angry protests from a large group of well-known people, including several members of the Academy itself (see Euskaltzaindia 1977).

Despite the opposition from within the Academy, supporters of standardisation continued to be very active. Two factors played in their favour. On the one hand, Mitxelena's presence and work ensured good progress. On the other, the Franciscan friar Luis Villasante had been appointed president of the Academy. He was a humble, hardworking, and intelligent person, always open to dialogue. Although not a linguist by training, he had ample knowledge of the language and had closely followed the progress towards standardisation. He had published several essays on the question: *Hacia la lengua literaria común* (Villasante 1970; "Towards the common literary language"), *La declinación del vasco literario común* (Villasante 1972; "The declension of common literary Basque"), and *La H en la ortografía vasca* (Villasante 1980; ("The H in Basque orthography").

Villasante was the right person for the job at that particular moment. He set up commissions within the Academy which, for the first time in its history, started working as a team. The most remarkable result was the standardisation of the auxiliary verb, in 1973. It was, without a doubt, the trickiest question, given the very different systems that different dialects used. Account was taken of the region in which each system was used and priority was given to those occupying a relatively large area. Where there was no clear ranking, the central forms were chosen. Generally speaking, difficulties were avoided, as a result of the application of wisdom and common sense (see Euskaltzaindia 1973).

The Congress of Bergara (1978)

After the Arantzazu Congress, the Academy of the Basque Language had set a period of ten years to evaluate the standardisation process. In 1978, it called a further congress in Bergara (Gipuzkoa), which adjudged that progress had indeed been made. Yes, there was strong opposition on the part of those who considered standardisation unnecessary and harmful, but most of the writers and teachers faithfully followed the dictates of the Academy. Encouraged and emboldened by the support it received, the Academy resolved to continue its work.

Some of those dissatisfied with the Academy's work had got together to set up an alternative body, Euskerazaintza. In 1983, Vicente Latiegi and Dionisio

Oñatibia published an essay titled *Euskaltzaindia, el batua y la muerte del euskera* ("Euskaltzaindia, the unified language, and the death of Basque"), setting out their ideas on standardisation (Latiegi and Oñatibia 1983):

> Basque is of the same species as the Greek. It is quadriform. It has four modalities: the eastern (Zuberoan-Roncalese), the northern (Lapurdian-Low Navarrese), the central (Navarrese-Gipuzkoan), and the western (Bizkaian). This pluriformity is essential to Basque. It has always been thus. For people of a Latinised mentality, this plurality is an inconvenience. For us, it is an advantage and a source of enrichment (p. 11).
>
> The *essential* unity of Basque, which is *essentially* a pluriform language, is that all Basques learn their own Basque modality (because they will certainly understand the other modalities). This unity of Basque *is perfected* by leaving the Basque language "untouched" as it is, pluriform, so that all Basques, as well as knowing their own modality, steep themselves to a certain extent in knowledge of the other modalities, so that they are capable not only of understanding them but of speaking them, or at least some of them (p. 112).[33]

These were the same ideas as those defended by Manuel Larramendi and Sabino Arana Goiri in the past; ideas that shocked at the end of the twentieth century.

Meanwhile, the official Academy, Euskaltzaindia, continued to work towards the establishment of a normative system. In the months that followed the Bergara Congress a number of accords were reached, relating mainly to morphology and spelling.

Regarding spelling, the ways in which *h* could be used were subjected to further regulation. From then on, its use was restricted to the start of words (*handi*, "big"), between vowels (*zahar*, "old"), and between diphthongs and vowels (*leiho*, "window") (Euskaltzaindia 1979b).

Regarding morphology, a decision was taken to be more flexible and to accommodate certain options that had been used since ancient times in many speech communities. This procedure broke with the rigidly hermetic approach followed until then. The following accords are noteworthy (Euskaltzaindia 1979a):

a   In the destinative case,* the endings -*entzat* and –*endako* were accepted: *lagunarentzat* and *lagunarendako*, "for the friend."

b   In the prolative case,* -*tzat* and the eastern -*tako: laguntzat* and *laguntako* "as a friend."

c   In the ablative* plural and the indefinite, -*etatik* and the early -*etarik: etxeetatik* and *etxeetarik*, "from (the) houses."

d   In the allative,* the variant -*rat* in the northern dialects was accommodated: *etxera* and *etxerat*, "to home."

e   In the allative of direction,* the Bizkaian -*rantz* was allowed (*etxerantz*, "towards home").

f   In declensions relating to animate beings, both *-gan* and the eastern *baitan* were accepted (*lagunarengan* and *lagunaren baitan*, "in the friend").

g   Finally, in the motivational,* the western *–tearren* was taken into account (*ikusteagatik* and *ikustearren*, "to see, in order to see").

In 1979, a Grammar Commission was set up, to work on standard Basque grammar. The first volume was published in 1985, *Euskal Gramatika: Lehen Urratsak* ("Basque grammar: First steps"; Euskaltzaindia 1985). Since then, a total of 11 volumes have been published.

The Congress of Leioa (1994)

In 1991, the Academy decided to revise the norms promulgated since 1968 and, at the same time, to intensify and speed up its work in that field. A congress was organised in 1994, to present and discuss the draft agreements. Once again, the Academy gained the support of important sectors of Basque society, in particular specialists and professionals in the field of language management.

The congress achieved two big breakthroughs. In the same year, 1994, the rules of the Academy, *Euskaltzaindiaren Arauak*, were made available to the public (Euskaltzaindia 1994). And in 1995 work started on a dictionary of standard Basque. The first draft arrived in 2000 and the second in 2008: *Hiztegi batua* ("Dictionary of standard Basque"; Euskaltzaindia 2008).

Standardisation: What has been achieved so far, and reflections for the future

Achievements

Nearly 60 years after the start of standardisation, we are now in a position to take stock. From a technical point of view, the process of standardisation of Basque has been a success. The enterprise began under the Franco dictatorship, with practically everything against it, including a lack of trained linguists to support it. The main exception was Koldo Mitxelena. Thanks to his engagement, and the enthusiastic support he received from the Academy, including people like Patxi Altuna, Gabriel Aresti, José Luis Alvarez Enparantza *Txillardegi*, and Luis Villasante, the project went from strength to strength. The achievements can be summarised in five points:

1   Standardisation has made it possible for speakers of different dialects to understand each other. Relations are now, for the most part, painless and relatively effortless.

2   Standardisation has made it possible for Basque to be incorporated into domains with which, hitherto, it has had little to do, or from which it has

been positively excluded, including teaching, administration, the media, and literature. True, it still has a long way to go before it achieves the same level as other languages, but the advances that it has made in little over half a century are meritorious and encouraging. Basque is now seen as on a par with the rest of the world's languages, and can be used in any field, given the right political will and economic resources.

3   Many people have been able to learn Basque, even in places where Basque is not widely spoken. They include people who live in areas from which Basque had previously disappeared or where it was never known to have been spoken, and even people in places far away from the Basque Country.

4   Standard Basque has helped overcome some of the serious problems caused by the administrative fragmentation of the Basque language community between France and Spain. Linguists and administrators are, at the very least, more knowledgeable about the problems and therefore better able to solve them.

5   Basque has gained in prestige. It is already seen as a language, and not just as a motley and disconnected set of dialects.

Challenges and tasks

The only really negative or at least debatable aspects of standardisation concern its manner of implementation. It happened rapidly and suddenly, and little distinction was made between Basque-speaking and non-Basque-speaking areas. Even in Basque-speaking areas, little distinction was made between those who used a dialect close to the standard model, as in Gipuzkoa and the western districts of Navarre, and those whose speech diverged significantly, for example in Zuberoa and Bizkaia. Instead, the same strategy and rhythm were adopted more or less indiscriminately.

There were, of course, reasons why this approach was taken. They can be summarised as follows:

a   Parts of the Basque Country were in a highly difficult political situation, under a regime of military dictatorship.

b   The definitive loss of Basque seemed imminent.

c   People felt strongly, one way or the other, about standardisation, leading to a radical polarisation into camps for and against. Some held that standard Basque would kill the dialects, so they opposed it. Others believed that the division into dialects would lead in a very short while to the death of the language, so many of them ignored and even repudiated the dialects.

One of the most serious consequences of this situation was that within many families the language was no longer transmitted. People thought that "good" Basque meant standard Basque, and that dialects were deficient.

Logically, therefore, large numbers were loath to pass on such a language to their children. They left everything to television and to school, areas newly conquered by Basque after a great struggle. Naturally, these instruments, although important, were not enough to guarantee a proper mastery of a language, which is why today many young people, even from Basque-speaking families, lack the command of Basque that might, in principle, have been assumed.

Not until after 1990 were voices heard saying that standard Basque and dialects could be complementary and not mutually antagonistic. Each should be allowed its proper space. In oral communication, especially in colloquial speech within each of the Basque-speaking areas, traditional dialects could be used.

However, the institutions remained silent. The Academy of the Basque Language, which since 1968 has led and managed the process of standardisation, did not explain which direction should be taken. Only in 2004 did it issue a statement accepting the use of dialects in certain domains. The statement was not just late in coming but added little new to the debate, apart from listing some of the experiences gained in previous years (see Euskaltzaindia 2004). In regard to education, so vital to the language, so far there seems to have been no official statement on this point. But a statement of direction is crucial, especially in the initial stages of standardisation, when dialects continue to retain much of their vitality and to enjoy the favour of important sectors of society.

A well-defined and well-delimited language model would specify usage, in textbooks, research work, media covering the Basque community as a whole, and the labelling and specifications of industrial products, food, textiles, pharmaceuticals, and so on.

In other fields, however, the standard model should be more flexible. For example, a general means of communication is not the same thing as a local one. A document issued by the Basque Government for all citizens is not the same as one issued by a local council. A university research paper is different from a local festival programme. While not opposing the use of standard Basque in all these areas, it seems to me that in places where traditional dialects have been kept alive, their special features should be honoured, particularly their vocabulary.

It is not uncommon for speakers of languages with deep dialect divisions across regions to express themselves in dialect both in public and in private. For example, Scottish standard English (or Scots) has a large number of words and phrases unrelated or only distantly related to their standard English equivalents, and some have been used for centuries in functional and communicative contexts, including legal and administrative discourse. Basque speakers should be allowed the same freedom. For example, they should be allowed to choose from competing variants such as *gabonak/eguberriak* ("Christmas"), *artaziak/guraizeak/aizturrak* ("scissors"), and *izara/maindire/mihise* ("sheet") in those places where such words are in popular usage.

Such a freedom would not lead, as some fear, to the fragmentation and or "Balkanisation" of Basque. It might even be the best way for speakers to identify more easily with the standard language and to accept it more readily. An excessively narrow and hermetic model, distant from ordinary speech in certain regions, leads speakers to see it as alien and to think twice before using it. There are many examples of this happening on the road to Basque standardisation.

From a linguistic point of view, variation is an essential characteristic of any language. As Juan Carlos Moreno Cabrera (2000) has shown, even a standard language will be realised in different ways by different speech communities. Variation is a feature of languages vital to their survival and absent only from dead or artificial languages that are not used as habitual means of communication in different communities. Rather than seek to impose one speech variety over others, society should promote and respect all varieties and allow them the space in which to develop and survive, even if one variety is, by general consensus, adopted as standard.

Notes

1 En la provincia hay un dialecto, que comparado con los demás puede decirse el mejor, más inteligible y gustoso, y pudiera dar testigos de esto en los otros dialectos, que así lo confiesan. Este dialecto es el único que por todas partes está rodeado de países bascongados, de Bizcaya, Alaba, Navarra, Labort, y por eso ha podido conservarse con más cultura y esplendor.

2 Gure izquera, beste bien erdicoa bezala, Nafarroan, baita Bizcaian ere gueiena aditcen da. Baña ez nafarrac Bizcaicoa, ta ez bizcaitarrac nafarrena aditcen dute: ta bata besteagandic urruti, ta bacoitza bere bidetic dabill.

3 Cuál de ellos debe ser preferido, yo no lo diré, porque sería disgustar a más de uno. Solo sé que el guipuzcoano es más afectuoso, y su tal cual ventaja consiste, en que así los vizcaínos, como los navarros le oyen con gusto, y le entienden, cuando por el contrario, no se entienden estos mutuamente.

4 Je choisirai mes exemples principalement dans le dialecte guipuscoan littéraire, comme étant le plus connu, le plus parlé, le plus cultivé, un des plus riches et des plus réguliers, et constituant, pour ainsi dire, le représentant légitime de la langue basque, à peu près au même titre que le toscan et le castillan représentent la langue italienne et l'espagnole.

5 Se forme una academia compuesta de los hombres más ilustrados del país bascongado, tanto franceses como españoles, que es de absoluta necesidad para los adelantos de nuestra lengua, y para que con el tiempo, modificando las diferencias de ortografía y pronunciación, y generalizando indistintamente las voces de los diferentes dialectos en la escritura y literatura, se forme una lengua común, comprensible para todas las provincias.

6 Sucede en todas estas poblaciones que miran con desdén al bascuence de Vizcaya y son muy apasionados al dialecto del Beterri: los sermones y pláticas se predican en ese dialecto de Beterri y muchísimas personas hacen estudio de este dialecto, por cuyo motivo hacen una mezcla; pero todavía no han podido *guipuzcoanizar* al vulgo.

7 Quand je dis biscayen et non pas guipuscoan de Vergara, je sais fort bien que cette manière de parler déplaît à Messieurs les Vergarais qui se piquent d'être de purs guipuscoans. Je ne dis pas non, de même que je ne nie pas que les sermons de leurs

curés les plus instruits et que souvent même le langage ordinaire des personnes les mieux élevées soient non seulement en guipuscoan, mais même dans la variété la plus pure de Beterri. Tout cela toutefois ne change en rien à ma manière de voir. Que les Vergarais aiment ou non les Biscayens et leur dialecte, il n'en est pas moins vrai que (...) cette variété vergaraise telle qu'elle est en usage parmi le bas peuple et les paysans, appartient linguistiquement parlant au biscayen oriental.

8 Siendo Bizkaya, por su raza, su lengua, su fe, su carácter y sus costumbres, hermana de Álaba, Benabarre, Gipuzkoa, Lapurdi, Nabarra y Suberoa, se ligará o confederará con estos seis pueblos para formar el todo llamado *Euskelerria* (Euskeria), pero sin mengua de su particular autonomía. Esta doctrina se expresa con el principio siguiente: *Bizkaya libre en Euskeria libre.*

9 Lo que procede, en mi opinión, es componer dentro de cada región euskeriana que haya sido antes estado autónomo y se halle en la posibilidad de volver a serlo algún día, un dialecto general, formado con los elementos menos alejados de las formas orgánicas, esparcidas aquí y allá, en los diferentes subdialectos o variedades que se hablen en el territorio de que se trate (...). De esta suerte tendríamos un solo euskera guipuzkoano, un solo euskera navarro, un solo euskera bizkaino, etc., viniendo a realizarse en la esfera lingüística la fórmula que en la política tiene tantos y tan decididos partidarios, *la variedad en la unidad.*

10 Nous essaierons de prouver que tous les livres basques imprimés jusqu'ici ont une orthographe vicieuse et barbare. Celle que nous proposons est applicable à la variété de tous les dialectes euskariens, et nous ferons ressortir ce qu'elle peut avoir de judicieux et de rationnel. [...] Faute d'Académie régulatrice, nos hommes instruits et le haut clergé, s'ils avaient encore un peu de patriotisme, devraient bien se concerter pour mettre un terme à l'anarchie qui règne dans cette partie de notre littérature nationale.

11 L'orthographe des textes basques que nous insérons est critiquée un peu à la légère par ceux qui ne se rendent pas bien compte de notre but. Il s'agit d'arrêter les règles de la meilleure orthographe pour l'universalité des dialectes euskariens. Plusieurs correspondants nous ont exposé leurs idées sur ce point, mais nous avons remarqué que la plupart, très-peu versés dans notre littérature nationale, semblent ignorer le système usité dans nos provinces espagnoles; ils ne sont préoccupés que de la routine suivie pour l'impression des livres de piété en dialecte labourdin.

12 Par une crainte, assez peu fondée, de n'être pas bien accueilli, le clergé ne se hasarde pas encore à la réforme, dans ses petits livres d'église.

13 L'abbé Jaurretche avait été le premier à comprendre la défectuosité de l'orthographe usitée le plus généralement et qui ne cessait de varier. Dans son *Mois de Marie*, il avait inséré une courte dissertation, pleine de vues très justes; et bien qu'il n'osât pas rompre avec les habitudes reçues, il avait néanmoins introduit dans ses livres quelques réformes. Des critiques malavisés lui en firent un crime; ils clabaudèrent de tous les côtés et firent même intervenir Mgr. l'Evêque pour forcer l'abbé Jaurretche à revenir sur les pas qu'il avait faits. Ce saint homme était plein d'humilité, ce qui n'empêchait pas qu'il ne vit clairement que le blanc n'était pas noir. Cependant il dut faire plusieurs concessions qui répugnaient à sa raison et son livre parut après cette longue lutte.

14 Jusqu'à ce que le prince Louis-Lucien fût venu dans nos contrées, chacun écrivait le basque à sa guise. Les divergences n'étaient pourtant pas considérables et il était facile de les ramener à l'unité. C'est ce dont le prince s'occupa; en grand philologue qu'il est. De là est venue l'orthographe rationnelle, que les auteurs adoptèrent aussitôt.

15 Aunque entre nosotros no hay todavía una academia de la lengua, la generalidad de los que en euskara escribimos, hemos adoptado, por considerarla la más conforme a su índole, la ortografía admitida y enseñada por mi esclarecido y generoso maestro, el por tantos méritos ilustre príncipe Luis Luciano Bonaparte. La *v* es

desconocida en nuestro alfabeto, así que sólo hacemos uso de la *b*. Empléase la *k* en sustitución de la *c* y *qu*. Usamos la *g* en *ge, gi*, con el mismo sonido que tiene en *ga, go, gu*. La *h* es desusada por considerársela inútil. Escríbese *z* en vez de *c* antes de *e, i*. Antes de *b* y *p* empleamos *n* en lugar de *m*, como igualmente usamos la *rr* en todos los casos de sonido fuerte, debiendo tenerse en cuenta que nunca va como sonido inicial, si no es precedido de una *e* por eufonía.

16   1ª ¿Sería conveniente el tender hacia la uniformidad de este idioma, a lo menos en su parte literaria?

2ª ¿Debería ser, en lo posible, absoluta esa uniformidad, o, por el contrario, habría de limitarse sólo a alguno o algunos de los elementos idiomáticos, como la fonética o el léxico, por ejemplo?

3ª ¿Qué medios podrían ponerse en práctica para llegar a la homogeneidad del euzkera literario? ¿Podría hacerse por un acuerdo entre todos los euzkeristas vascos, o sería necesario proceder por lenta evolución de las formas literarias actuales?

4ª El euzkera literario homogéneo ¿sería uno de los actuales dialectos adoptado con preferencia a los demás, aunque con elementos gramaticales de todos ellos, o bien sería un lenguaje, en cierto modo nuevo, formado con elementos de todos los dialectos, pero sin influencia preponderante de ninguno de ellos?

17   No puedo coincidir en esta opinión con el gran escritor patriota. Si ha de haber un euzkera guipuzkoano, otro nabarro, otro bizkaino, etc., toda literatura euzkeldun es imposible: es cuestión de hechos positivos, y no ha menester de demostración. (...) Creo que la aspiración general es, hoy, a la uniformidad, por lo menos en el euzkera literario.

18   Para mí, la unificación a base del dialecto guipuzkoano, adoptado desde ahora como literario, es la solución más práctica: el guipuzkoano es un dialecto vivo, hablado por mayor número de personas que cualquier otro, el más céntrico de todos, el más afín de los demás dialectos y el de mayor influencia sobre todos; además tengo entendido que literariamente es y ha sido el más cultivado. Y conste que no soy guipuzkoano, ni tengo ascendencia guipuzkoana conocida; pero creo que ningún dialecto puede disputar a aquél la primacía.

19   Tendremos que resolver, necesariamente, la cuestión de los dialectos (...). Pensar que un pequeño pueblo de medio millón de almas, casi analfabeto, muy poco aficionado a leer, pueda permitirse el lujo de poseer tres o cuatro dialectos literarios, equivale desde luego a negar toda posibilidad de culturalidad euzkérica. Esos tres o cuatro dialectos literarios no servirán más que para trazar el elocuentísimo epitafio del idioma común, víctima desdichada de tan nefastos lujos. (...) Reconozco desde ahora que el renacimiento literario de la lengua está absolutamente condicionado por la adopción de un dialecto único y uniforme para lo escrito y aun para lo oral literario.

20   Esa diversidad de dialectos, subdialectos y variedades, se ha mantenido por dos principales circunstancias, que son: la falta de una literatura tradicional escrita, y el desdichado fraccionamiento político en que durante toda su historia ha vivido la nación vasca.

21   El estudio del euzkera para los erdeldunes resulta, por la misma razón de la diversidad de dialectos y subdialectos, incomparablemente ingrato e inútil; lo que aprendieron a oír, a decir, no les servirá sin nuevos esfuerzos, más que en contados pueblos.

22   Comparando unos dialectos con otros, desde luego tendremos que descartar al *zuberuano*, variedad extrema de la lengua, como extremo es su territorio y falto de comunicación con el resto del país, y lo mismo tendremos que hacer con el *labur-dino* no obstante su mayor afinidad con los dialectos peninsulares; esta afinidad está muy perjudicada por la invasión francesa, la carencia de centros de vida euzkeldunes y, en resumen, por la evidente falta de influjo del euzkera laburdino

sobre los demás (…). Reducida la cuestión de primacía a los euzkeras bizcaino y
vascón (o guipuzcoano), hay que reconocer que la mayor parte de las ventajas
están por éste. Ni el número de habitantes que habla actualmente el bizkaino
admite comparación con el de los euzkeldunes que hablan el guipuzcoano, ni la
calidad de la población, labradora o pescadora casi toda en Bizcaya, ni la impor-
tancia de las villas o pueblos en que el bizkaino se habla.

23 Lenguas vivas existen sin el menor vestigio de literatura. La historia conocida del
euzkera, historia es de una lengua que en sus largos siglos de vida no ha producido
literatura apreciable. Y ¿por esto ha llegado a trance de muerte? No, ciertamente,
sino por falta de verdadera conciencia nacional, de verdadero patriotismo.

Achacar a diversidad de dialectos la muerte del euzkera es andarse por las
ramas. Pretender evitar esa muerte con la desaparición de sus dialectos es querer
curar la enfermedad aplicando la medicina en la parte sana y no en la enferma.
Digamos con el Maestro y digamos de una vez para siempre: el euzkera por el
euzkera morirá; el euzkera por la patria perdurará.

24 Se deduce que por el estudio comparativo de los dialectos comprobó Sabino que el
bizkaino es el que más se acerca al euzkera primitivo, el más uniforme, el más rico
en la fonética y en el verbo y el más radicalmente pospositivo.

25 According to the myth established by Augustin Chaho, Aitor was the father of the
Basques.

26 Si Demóstenes o Píndaro hubieran hoy de escribir en la lengua de Aitor,
escogerían el uno para sus arengas y el otro para sus vehementes odas, el seco
dialecto vizcaíno, o tomarían de él la mayor dosis, sazonando su lenguaje con
elementos de los otros en menor escala; si Lisias, Sócrates o Cicerón, se me
ocurre que tomarían por base el guipuzcoano; si en fin Anacreonte, Luciano el
filósofo o Aristófanes sus gracias y sátiras, no concibo que hallaran base más
apta que el pirenaico. (…) Ésa es la norma que me parece más acertada, y
ninguno tan apto para realizarla que el mismo escritor.

27 Figurémonos que eso, que yo estimo imposible, se realizara, y que las nuevas
generaciones del pueblo vasco llegaran a aprender la lengua artificiosa unificada.
Pues la Academia, en vez de haber continuado, depurado e impulsado el vasco
histórico, como es su misión, habría roto bruscamente la tradición en el desarrollo
del idioma, para lanzar a éste en una vía nueva; habría quitado a la lengua la
mayor parte de su valor y de su autoridad histórica; habría matado a los venerables
dialectos tradicionales, consagrados por la adhesión fervorosa de las generaciones
vascas de hace muchos siglos, y los habría sacrificado en aras de un producto nuevo,
desprovisto de interés arqueológico y sin utilidad alguna para la cultura humana,
hecho sólo para el pueril interés de poder decir en una lengua exótica lo que muy
bien puede decirse en cualquiera de las dos grandiosas lenguas culturales del
extremo occidental de Europa.

28 En vascuence no se puede pensar con universalidad. Y el pueblo vasco, cuando se
eleva a la universalidad, lo hace en español o en francés. (…) Los autores del
Informe conocen y reconocen la pobreza del vascuence vivo para expresar los
múltiples aspectos de la vida moderna; saben de sobra que no se podría explicar en
vascuence ni química, ni física, ni psicología, ni… ciencia alguna. Saben de sobra
que el vocabulario religioso o teológico y psicológico del vascuence es de origen
latino.

29 Izkelgiz gipuzkoarrak yaio diranei oartxo bat egin nai nieke bukatu baño len.
Guipuzkoarrak erakutsi digute ontan ere targorik zoroena. Akademiak aspaldi
erabaki zun aditz laguntzallean *dut, duzu* ta urrengoak erabiltzeko, *det* eta *dot*-en
ordez. Orra, gipuzkoarrak oraindik agindu aditzeratara malgutzeke; beti ere beren
zorigaiztoko *det* erabilki agertzen zaizkigu. […] Yaunak, zuek ere ikasi ezazute
zuenetik zerbait uzten batasunaren onerako. Besteok askoz ere erauzketa aundi ta
mingarriagoak egin bear izan ditugu zuen izkelgi ederrari indar emateko.

30 Labayen was referring to some declarations made by Luis Haranburu Altuna (1972: 10–11) concerning *h:* "In the years 1960–64 there has been a rupture that affects both the depths and the form. As far as language is concerned, the symbol of the rupture is the letter *h*. All revolutions have their symbolism and, in our history, that symbol is *h*."

31 Por las propias declaraciones de sus autores sabemos que tomaron la *Hache* por símbolo de sus propósitos que son los de destruir la obra cultural realizada en los cincuenta años anteriores. Y principalmente, en lo que tiene de sentido tradicional, de adhesión a la fe religiosa de nuestros mayores; minando sus modos de vida, sus costumbres y su organización familiar. Es el odio al cristianismo y no la conciencia de un justo socialismo lo que les impulsa en su obsesión teórica-revolucionaria, *¡IRAULTZA!* a la negación de los valores del tesoro moral y espiritual de nuestro pueblo. No hay sino leer los libros y folletos que van publicando en sus colecciones; los artículos de sus periódicos y revistas, plagadas casi todos de obscenidades y fraseología marxistoide. Eso sí bajo capa de *"batasuna"* y profusión de *"haches"*.

32 La *h* es un símbolo político aunque lo nieguen muy sesudos señores, aunque vayan investidos de seráficos hábitos. Tan político como pueda ser la hoz y el martillo, la cruz gamada o las dos a la vez.

La ortografía achista no es más que un intento de politizar el euskera, rompiendo los moldes tradicionales, como una rama más de lo que se intenta romper: la familia, el derecho a la educación cristiana, nuestras costumbres peculiares, nuestra personalidad, etc., como medio para conseguir una juventud sin moral, sin sentimientos, ni conciencia de pertenecer a un pueblo con unas costumbres discutibles pero indudablemente mejores de las que nos proponen a juzgar por las muestras que vemos.

33 El euskera es de la misma especie que el griego. Es cuatriforme. Cuatro son sus modalidades: el oriental (suletino-roncalés), el septentrional (laburdino-benabarrés), el central (navarro-guipuzcoano) y el occidental (vizcaíno). Esa pluriformidad es esencial al euskera. Siempre ha sido así: cuatriforme. Para gentes de mentalidad latinizada esa pluriformidad es un inconveniente. Para nosotros es una ventaja y una riqueza.

La unidad *esencial* del euskera que *esencialmente* es lengua pluriforme, consiste en que cada vasco aprenda su propia modalidad euskérica, (porque ya, sin más, comprenderá las otras modalidades). Esa unidad del euskera *se perfecciona* dejando "intocada" a la lengua tal cual es, pluriforme, y haciendo que cada vasco, además de conocer bien su propia modalidad, profundice un poco en el conocimiento de las otras modalidades, para que sea capaz no sólo de entenderlas sino de hablarlas, al menos alguna de ellas.

References

Aizkibel, José Francisco. 1884. *Diccionario bilingüe*. Tolosa: Eusebio López.

Altuna, Patxi (ed.). 1987. "Duvoisinen eskuizkribu argitaragabea". *Fontes Linguae Vasconum*, 29, nº 49, 65–95. Iruña: Institución Príncipe de Viana.

Alvarez Enparantza, José Luis (Txillardegi). 1994. *Euskal Herria helburu*. Tafalla: Txalaparta.

Arana, José Ignacio. 1872. *San Ignacio Loyolacoaren bicitza laburtua euskaraz eta gaztelaniaz*. Bilbao: Larumbe anayen moldizteguia.

Arana, José Ignacio. 1895. *Complementos a la Obra de Averiguaciones Cantábricas e Ignacianas, del P. Gabriel de Henao de la Compañía de Jesús* (VI) (First complement, sixth appendix). Tolosa: E. López.

Arana Goiri, Sabino. 1894. "Euskeldun Batzokija". Reprinted in *Obras Completas de Sabino Arana Goiri* (I): 279–291. Donostia: Sendoa, 1980.

Arana Goiri, Sabino. 1896. *Lecciones de ortografía del euskera bizkaino*. Reprinted in *Obras Completas de Sabino Arana Goiri* (II): 810–982. Donostia: Sendoa, 1980.

Arenaza, Josu. 1974. *Tus hijos y el euskera. (El mito del "batua")*. Bilbao: La Editorial Vizcaina.

Aresti, Gabriel. 1959. *Maldan behera*. Reprinted in *Obra guztiak* (I): 178–335. Donostia: Kriselu, 1976.

Azkue, Resurrección M. 1896. *Proyecto de ortografía*. Bilbao: Müller y Zavaleta.

Azkue, Resurrección M. 1917. *Prontuario fácil para el estudio de la lengua vasca*. 2ª edition, Bilbao: Editorial Vasca, 1932.

Azkue, Resurrección M. 1918. *Ardi galdua*. Bilbao: Jesusen Biotzaren elaztegian.

Azkue, Resurrección M. 1934–1935. "Gipuzkera osotua". *Euskera*, 15: 1–150 and 16: 151–184. Bilbao: Academia de la Lengua Vasca.

Basterretxea, José (Oskillaso). 1962. *Kurloiak*. Zarautz: Itxaropena.

Belaustegigoitia, Federico. 1916. *La unificación del euzkera*. Bilbao: J. Echenagusia.

Bonaparte, Louis-Lucien. 1869. *Le verbe basque en tableaux, accompagné de notes grammaticales, selon les huit dialectes de l'euskara*. Reprinted in (J. A. Arana Martija, ed.) *Opera omnia vasconice* (I): 221–442. Bilbao: Real Academia de la Lengua Vasca, 1991.

Campión, Arturo. 1880. "Gramática Euskara". *Revista Euskara*, 3. Iruña.

Campión, Arturo and Pierre Broussain. 1922. "Informe de los señores académicos A. Campión y P. Broussain a la Academia de la Lengua Vasca sobre unificación del euskera". *Euskera*, 3–1: 4–17. Bilbao.

d'Abbadie, Antoine Th. and J. Augustin Chaho. 1836. *Études grammaticales sur la langue euskarienne*. Paris: Arthus Bertrand.

Daranatz, Jean-Baptiste (ed.). 1928–1931. "Correspondance du Capitaine Duvoisin". *Revista Internacional de Estudios Vascos*, 19–22. Reprinted in Bilbao: La Gran Enciclopedia Vasca, 1972.

Darrigol, Jean-Pierre. 1827. *Dissertation critique et apologétique sur la langue basque*. Baiona: Duhart-Fauvet.

Duhalde, Martin. 1809. *Meditacioneac gei premiatsuenen gainean, cembait abisuekin, othoitcekin eta bicitceco erregela batekin*. Baiona: Cluzeau anayen baithan.

Eleizalde, Koldobika. 1911. "Raza, Lengua y Nación vascas". *Euzkadi*, 8–10, 243–276.

Eleizalde, Koldobika. 1919a. *La lucha por el idioma propio*. Bilbao: Bilbaína de Artes Gráficas.

Eleizalde, Koldobika. 1919b. "Metodología para la restauración del euzkera". *Primer Congreso de Estudios Vascos*: 428–439. Bilbao: Bilbaína de Artes Gráficas.

Euskaltzaindia (Real Academia de la Lengua Vasca). 1922. "Euskararen batasunaz izan diran batzaldietan irakurritako txosten edo ikerpenak". *Euskera*, 3, 1–132.

Euskaltzaindia (Real Academia de la Lengua Vasca). 1968. "Arantzazuko Biltzarrak". *Euskera*, 13, 137–265.

Euskaltzaindia (Real Academia de la Lengua Vasca). 1973. "Aditz laguntzaile batua". *Euskera*, 18, 5–74.

Euskaltzaindia (Real Academia de la Lengua Vasca). 1977. "Zenbait Euskaltzaindikok eginiko gutuna". *Euskera*, 22–1, 207–208.

Euskaltzaindia (Real Academia de la Lengua Vasca). 1979a. "Deklinabidea". *Euskera*, 24–2, 633–657.

Euskaltzaindia (Real Academia de la Lengua Vasca). 1979b. "H letraren ortografi arauak". *Euskera*, 24–2, 659–695.

Euskaltzaindia (Real Academia de la Lengua Vasca). 1985-. *Euskal Gramatika: Lehen urratsak* (11 vols). Bilbao.
Euskaltzaindia (Real Academia de la Lengua Vasca). 1994-. *Euskaltzaindiaren Arauak*. Bilbao.
Euskaltzaindia (Real Academia de la Lengua Vasca). 2004. "Adierazpena euskalkien erabileraz irakaskuntzan, komunikabideetan eta Administrazioan". *Euskaltzaindiaren arauak* (iii): 1347–1350. Bilbao.
Euskaltzaindia (Real Academia de la Lengua Vasca). 2008. *Hiztegi Batua*. Donostia: Euskaltzaindia and Elkar.
Euzkeltzale-Bazkuna. 1916. *Sobre la unificación del euzkera*. Bilbao-Abando: Grijelmo.
Haranburu Altuna, Luis. 1972. *Euskal Literatura 72*. Donostia: Lur.
Hualde, José Ignacio and Koldo Zuazo. 2007. "The standardization of the Basque language". *Language Problems & Language Planning*. Amsterdam: John Benjamin Publishing Company 31:2, 143–168.
Ibiñagabeitia, Andima. 1952. "Kultur bidean". *Gernika*, nº 21, 237–239. Donibane Lohizune.
Ikabalzeta. 1910. "Una contestación". *Euzkadi*, 7, nº 4, 295–300.
Iza, Luis. 1881. *Zalameako alkatia*. Bilbao: Juan E. Delmas.
Jakin. 1965. "Baionako Biltzarraren Erabakiak". *Jakin*, 18, 20–28.
Jauretxe, Jean. 1838. *Andre-dena Mariaren ilhabethea, edo Maihatza Jaincoaren amaren loriacotz contsecratua*. Baiona: Cluzeau.
Kardaberatz, Agustín. 1761. *Eusqueraren berri onac*. Reprinted in *Obras completas de Agustín de Kardaberaz* (i): 153–170. Bilbao: La Gran Enciclopedia Vasca, 1973.
Labayen, Antonio M.ª 1972. *"Sasi-batasuna". Mala letra y peor espíritu de una pseudo unificación*. Tolosa: Lopez-Mendizabal.
Larramendi, Manuel. 1745. *Diccionario trilingüe del castellano, bascuence y latín*. Donostia: Bartolomé Riesgo y Montero.
Latiegi, Vicente and Dionisio Oñatibia. 1983. *Euskaltzaindia, el batua y la muerte del euskera*. Donostia: Lorea Artes Gráficas.
Manterola, José. 1880. "Algunas observaciones sobre ortografía vasca". *Cancionero vasco*. Serie iii. Donostia.
Menéndez Pidal, Ramón. 1920. "Introducción al estudio de la lingüística vasca". Reprinted in *En torno a la lengua vasca*: 11–57. Buenos Aires: Espasa-Calpe, 1962.
Mitxelena, Koldo. 1962. "Kurloiak (Herri txoriak)". *Egan*, 20, nº 4-6, 304–305. Donostia: Diputación Foral de Gipuzkoa.
Mogel, Juan Antonio. 1987. *Cristauaren icasbidea edo doctrina cristiania*. (L. Villasante, ed.) Bilbao: Real Academia de la Lengua Vasca.
Moreno Cabrera, Juan Carlos. 2000. *La dignidad e igualdad de las lenguas. Crítica de la discriminación lingüística*. Madrid: Alianza.
Ormaetxea, Nikolas (Orixe). 1920. "Unificación del lenguaje literario. Diversas soluciones". *Revista Internacional de Estudios Vascos*, 11: 53–61. Reprinted in Bilbao: La Gran Enciclopedia Vasca, 1969.
Ruiz de Larrinaga, Juan (ed.). 1954–1958. "Cartas del P. Uriarte al Príncipe Luis Luciano Bonaparte". *Boletín de la Real Sociedad Vascongada de los Amigos del País*, 10: 231–302, 13: 220–239, 330–348, 429–452 and 14: 397–443. Donostia: Diputación Foral de Gipuzkoa.
Unamuno, Miguel. 1920. "La unificación del vascuence". Reprinted in *Obras Completas* (vi): 344–348. Madrid: Afrodisio Aguado, 1958.

Urkijo, Julio. 1908–1910. "Cartas escritas por el príncipe L. L. Bonaparte a algunos de sus colaboradores". *Revista Internacional de Estudios Vascos*, 2: 215–221, 655–659 and 4: 235–297. Reprinted in Bilbao: La Gran Enciclopedia Vasca, 1969.

Villasante, Luis. 1963. "Oskillasoren Kurloiak". Revista *Aranzazu*, 416: 62. Oñati.

Villasante, Luis. 1970. *Hacia la lengua literaria común*. Oñati: Editorial Franciscana.

Villasante, Luis. 1972. *La declinación del vasco literario común*. Oñati: Editorial Franciscana.

Villasante, Luis. 1980. *La H en la ortografía vasca*. Oñati: Editorial Franciscana.

Glossary

Anaptictic vowel or anaptixis   is the adding of a vowel, usually copying the following one, to break up a group of consonants of the *muta cum liquida* type, i.e., an occlusive (sometimes including [*f*]) followed by a liquid [*l* or *r*]). In Basque, it is frequent in borrowings from Latin, at least in cases where the liquid is *-r-*: *liburu* (*<librum*), *garazi* (*<gratia*), *gurutz* (*<crux*), *daraturu* (*<taladrum*), *boronde* (*<frontem*).

Cases   It is usually maintained that Basque has a case system. The suffixes used where Spanish or French would use prepositions can be considered as postpositions agglutinated at the end of the noun phrase: *etxe berri-a* ("the/a new house"), *etxe berri-tik* ("from the new house"), *etxe berri-eta-tik* ("from the new houses"), *etxe berri-rako* ("for the new house"), *etxe berri-a-gatik* ("because of the new house"), *etxe berri-a-z* ("of/about the new house"). Here are some of the cases cited in this book:

Ablative   indicates provenance, as in *etxetik dator* ("comes from home"), or the place of transit, as in *Pisuerga ibaia Valladolidetik pasatzen da* ("the Pisuerga River passes through Valladolid").

Absolutive   or zero marking. They apply both to the direct objects of absolutive-ergative verbs (cf. i) and the subjects of verbs of the absolutive type (cf. ii):

    i. *Maradonak Fidel Castro agurtu zuen* ("Maradona greeted Fidel Castro")

    ii. *Maradona kazetariekin haserretu zen* ("Maradona was angry with the journalists")

Allative   indicates the place to which one goes: *etxera doa* ("he/she goes home"). *Allative of direction* indicates the place towards which you are going: *etxerantz doa* ("goes towards home").

Comitative or sociative   indicates, in general, company: *lagunarekin doa* ("goes with the friend"). However, in many cases it is only a suffix ruled by the verb: *Maradona kazetariekin haserretu zen* ("Maradona was angry with the journalists"), *Jon Asierrekin ezkonduko da* ("Jon will get married with Asier"). It may also have an instrumental value: *erosketak VISA txartelarekin ordaindu ditut* ("I made the purchases with a VISA card").

Dative   The dative suffix is usually associated with interpretations of goal/target or benefactive/malefactive, depending on the verb: *Joni telegrama bat heldu zaio* ("a telegram has arrived for Jon"), *Joni lore sorta bat* *oparitu diot* ("I gave a bunch of flowers to Jon as a present"). There are also names or phrases that govern the dative: *Joni begira* ("looking at Jon").

Destinative   indicates for whom: *lagunarentzat erosi du* ("has bought it for his/her friend").

Ergative   marks the subject of transitive verbs, of the ergative-absolutive or ergative-absolutive-dative type: *Maradonak Fidel Castro agurtu zuen* ("Maradona greeted Fidel Castro").

Genitive   A distinction is usually made between the possessive (*-en*) and the locative (*-ko*). The first is usually linked to the expression of possession, but often simply marks the relationship of the subject or object of a noun, as in English:

 i. *Jonen etxea* ("Jon's house")

 ii. *Arestiren itzulpenak* ("Aresti's translations"; Aresti can be the translator or the translated).

The so-called locative genitive typically expresses place or origin with respect to a noun iii, but sometimes it introduces a noun modifier or a complement governed by it:

 iii. *Donostiako Kursaal jauregia* ("The Kursaal Palace of [i.e., in] Donostia")

 iv. *hiru urteko ardoa* ("a wine of three years" [i.e., three years old])

 v. *fisikako ikaslea* ("physics student")

Inessive   indicates where something is: *etxean dago* ("is at home").

Motivative   indicates the cause or reason: *zu ikusteagatik etorri naiz* ("I have come to see you").

Prolative   is the suffix used in some cases of predication, whose English equivalent could be "for": *Jon laguntzat hartu dute* ("they have taken Jon for a friend"), *eskuizkribua galdutzat jotzen zuten* ("they gave the manuscript up for lost").

Deitic adverbs   are those formed on the basis of the demonstratives. They are of place, like *hemen, hor, han* ("here, there [near], there [distant]") and their variants, or of manner, like *honela, horrela, hala* ("thus, in this way, in that way" etc.)

Verbs of an absolutive type   (known as the NOR type in Basque grammars). They select a single absolutive noun phrase or NOR and use the auxiliary *izan* ("to be"). For example: *Aitor Estatu Batuetan bizi da* ("Aitor lives in the United States"), *Aitor Chicagon jaio zen* ("Aitor was born in Chicago").

Verbs of the absolutive-dative type   (known as the NOR-NORI type). They take two NPs, one dative and one absolutive, and are conjugated with the auxiliary *izan* ("to be"). For example: *Amaiari loteria tokatu zaio* ("Amaia has won the lottery"), *Amaia txakurrari hurbildu zitzaion* ("Amaia approached the dog").

Verbs of the absolutive-dative-ergative type   (known as the NOR-NORI-NORK type). They select three NPs, with the cases mentioned and the auxiliary usually considered as a variant of the verb *edun* ("to have"). For example: *Mirenek amari lore sorta eman zion* ("Miren gave his mother a bouquet of flowers").

Verbs of the absolutive-ergative type (known as the NOR-NORK type). They usually select two noun phrases, one absolutive and one ergative, and take the auxiliary *edun* ("to have"): *Jonek ABC egunkaria irakurtzen du* ("Jon is reading the *ABC* newspaper").

Index